Chinese Theatre

Many colorful theatrical activities can be found throughout China. The best-known and most unique of these is perhaps traditional Chinese opera, which has a history of over 800 years. However, since the early twentieth century, following increased contact with the West, drama without music has also become popular in China. The development and prosperity of modern drama has created a new landscape for Chinese theatre, which, as a whole, has become more diverse. In this illustrated introduction Fu Jin explores the origins and development of this distinctive branch of the Chinese arts.

Introductions to Chinese Culture

The thirty volumes in the Introductions to Chinese Culture series provide accessible overviews of particular aspects of Chinese culture written by a noted expert in the field concerned. The topics covered range from architecture to archaeology, from mythology and music to martial arts. Each volume is lavishly illustrated in full color and will appeal to students requiring an introductory survey of the subject, as well as to more general readers.

Fu Jin

CHINESE THEATRE

CAMBRIDGE
UNIVERSITY PRESS

CAMBRIDGE
UNIVERSITY PRESS

University Printing House, Cambridge CB2 8BS, United Kingdom

One Liberty Plaza, 20th Floor, New York, NY 10006, USA

477 Williamstown Road, Port Melbourne, VIC 3207, Australia

314-321, 3rd Floor, Plot 3, Splendor Forum, Jasola District Centre, New Delhi - 110025, India

79 Anson Road, #06-04/06, Singapore 079906

Cambridge University Press is part of the University of Cambridge.

It furthers the University's mission by disseminating knowledge in the pursuit of
education, learning and research at the highest international levels of excellence.

www.cambridge.org
Information on this title: www.cambridge.org/9780521186667

Originally published by China Intercontinental Press as
The Art of Chinese Theatre (9787508516837) in 2010

© China Intercontinental Press 2010

This updated edition is published by Cambridge University Press
with the permission of China Intercontinental Press under
the China Book International programme ◢●◝.

For more information on the China Book International programme, please visit
http://www.cbi.gov.cn/wisework/content/10005.html

Cambridge University Press retains copyright in its own contributions
to this updated edition

© Cambridge University Press 2012

First published 2012

A catalogue record for this publication is available from the British Library

ISBN 978-0-521-18666-7 Paperback

Contents

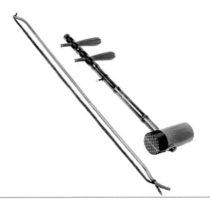

Foreword

Of all of China's diverse theatrical traditions, traditional Chinese opera is perhaps the most unique. Originating in the twelfth century, traditional Chinese opera has a rich history and an enchanting style which remains popular today. The music and singing follow set rhythmical patterns and characters' speech is based on particular poetic meters. In operas about wars, the rhythm of marital arts is used to evoke battle scenes.

Actors preparing ready backstage.

Singing, speech, movement and acrobatic fighting are the four basic methods used in the performance of traditional Chinese opera, which is a form of physical theatre. Other than perhaps a simple table, two chairs and a few essential props, performances take place through the use of the techniques of physical theatre, as well as monologues and dialogues. To represent going upstairs, for example, an actor might mime the action by lifting their clothes and legs. To represent doors and windows, actors might use their bodies to create these objects. Other examples include snapping a whip to represent horse-riding, paddling with an oar to signify sailing and moving in a circle to represent traveling around mountains or through water. These techniques mean that traditional Chinese opera has a versatile and flexible form. Performances can move location easily and narratives can be changed freely. Every move the actors make on stage, be it a smile or a frown, can be rich in meaning, vividly reflecting the inner emotions of the characters.

The extensive use of music in traditional Chinese opera reinforces the lyrical nature of the form, which is particularly suitable for portraying intricate and nuanced psychological changes of characters facing complex situations. Typically, the main characters are assigned most of the singing, especially in the central scenes, where changes in rhythm reflect changes in emotion. Certain performers often become popular because of their

The Ancient Peking Opera Garden.

singing ability and their unique way of expressing feelings. In fact, individual performance styles have, at times, helped to shape different operatic genres.

Traditional Chinese opera uses costumes based on the dress of historical figures from the Ming Dynasty (1368–1644). Make-up is often intense in color. Some male characters wear masks with exaggerated shapes or symbolic colors. A red-faced mask means justice, a black one signifies bluntness, while a white mask symbolizes treachery.

Love stories are a perpetual theme on the Chinese theatrical stage.

Although operas may be distinguished from each other on the basis of the style of the singing, speaking, movement and acrobatic fighting, operatic forms can be differentiated first and foremost by differences in the melodies and musical instruments they employ. These differences arose due to the many local languages and dialects which existed across China's vast territory. Opera performers had to use dialects which their audiences would understand, and these dialects influenced the style of the melody. There were once 300 different operatic forms in China and about 200 still exist today, showcasing China's rich and diverse array of theatrical styles.

From the beginning of the twentieth century, and as a result of Western influences, modern drama and stage plays (without

There are two main types of traditional Chinese opera: lyric operas and acrobatic operas which include stage fighting.

singing) appeared in China. For more than 100 years, modern drama has gradually been integrated into Chinese culture and its development and prosperity has signaled a new era for Chinese theatre, which, as a whole, continues to diversify.

Introduction: The Origins of Chinese Theatre

Sacrificial Entertainments

The origins of Chinese theatre can be traced back 2,500 years. At the beginning of Chinese civilization, shamen in tribal and ethnic groups held considerable power. Sacrificial ritual music and dance performances were considered ways in which shamen could communicate with the gods, and acted as a channel between the gods and man, thus unifying the human and spiritual worlds. Early Chinese theatre developed from, and was closely related to, these sacrificial ceremonies.

Whilst basic theatrical forms had been present from the beginning of Chinese civilization, a more developed theatre did not emerge until the tenth century, thousands of years later than the theatres of ancient Greece and ancient India. In ancient China, theatrical performances consisted of symbolic story-telling by actors dressed as animals who danced and sang to set rhythms, accompanied by music. Poems, especially those based on the folk songs of *The Book of Songs* (China's earliest collection of poetry, which appeared between 770–476 BC), were performed by singing and dancing, fusing the emotional effects of literature with those of music and movement. Sacrificial rituals in the southern state of Chu during the Warring States Period (475–256 BC) also provided opportunities for performance. The famous poet of the Chu Period, Qu Yuan (340–278 BC), produced

These bronze chime bells of the Warring States Period were the main musical instruments used in the sacrificial ceremonies held by the imperial family and noblemen.

The musical tower of the City God's temple of the Tang Dynasty, a place where theatre was performed and sacrifices offered.

several volumes of poetry including *Nine Songs and Nine Chapters*, which were adapted for performance at sacrificial ceremonies. "National Martyr" from *Nine Songs*, which describes the memorial ceremony for the national martyrs, was one such adaptation. A large number of Chu poems circulated in southern China and set a basic pattern for large-scale sacrificial ceremonies, where poetry was sung and accompanied by dancing. Although these ceremonies could not be described as "theatre" in a classic sense, they contained all the elements required for theatrical performance. In addition, the comic performances of jesters and entertainers at the courts of the vassal states might also be considered as early forms of theatre.

The Development of Music and Dance

Rapid social development during the Han Dynasty (202 BC–AD 220) signaled a new phase for theatre, both at court and in civil society. The ancient Chinese usually prayed for a good harvest

A figurine of a comic entertainer during the Han Dynasty.

in springtime and gave thanks in the autumn, which is why ritual singing and dancing at these times was vital, both at court and among common people. The court held large performances for the general public, which, to a certain extent, stimulated town and country entertainments and allowed for the decentralization of theatrical performances. Whilst the royal sacrificial ceremony was highly standardized, in towns and rural areas entertainments gradually evolved through folk artists who made a living from their performances. Assisted by increasing trade between China and the west, singing, dancing and acrobatics from the western regions of China spread to Chang'an (present-day Xi'an) and the political center of the Han also became a global center for multi-cultural entertainment.

Following the Han Dynasty, music and dance developed significantly. The folk song and dance performance *ta-yao-niang* first appeared during the Northern Qi Dynasty (550–577)

Brick carvings of theatrical characters during the Han Dynasty.

A Dunhuang mural painting depicting scenes of music and dance from the Tang Dynasty.

This painting, entitled *A Musical Scene from the Palace*, depicts maids in a palace of the Tang Dynasty enjoying a feast and playing music.

and developed during the Tang Dynasty (618–907). *Ta-yao-niang* is a family saga. It tells the tale of a woman, bullied at home by her drunken husband, who repeatedly tells passers-by about her miserable life, as her husband beats her in public. The female lead would perform through song, dance and speech, whilst together with a jester the actress would perform a song-and-dance duet (*er ren zhuan*). The popularity of song and dance forms like *Ta-yao-niang*, *Su-mu-zhe*, *Lan-ling-wang* and *Bo-tou* peaked during the Sui (581–618) and Tang dynasties. In Dunhuang it is possible see many murals from that time which depict the busy and flourishing theatrical life of the era.

Xinong and the Art of "Singing with Speaking"

Canjun Opera was the most advanced form of early comic theatre in China. It had at its core two roles, the person being mocked, "canjun," and the person doing the mocking, "canghu." However by the end of the Tang Dynasty, Canjun Opera had evolved to include more performers and more complex plots and dramatic twists. Canjun Opera combined comedy with tragedy, and had a direct impact on the creation of *zaju* during the Song (960–1279) and Jin (1115–1234) dynasties. Canjun Opera was mostly improvised, allowing for constant innovation in the creation of comic routines. Occasional, impromptu performances gradually became regular shows that were staged during the Tang, Song and Jin dynasties.

Mural from a tomb found in Henan Province depicting music and dance from the Song Dynasty.

Xinong was influenced by Canjun Opera (an early form of Song Jin *zaju*) and developed from the comic performances of entertainers at court. Song Jin *zaju* drew on a great deal of this material, so that even after Xinong was replaced by a more advanced form of theatre, its short, comic forms remained an integral part of modern theatre.

During the Tang and Song dynasties, large cities such as Chang'an, Kaifeng and Hangzhou had prosperous economies that promoted the large-scale development of the entertainment industry. A variety of performance-

A painting entitled *Children Watching an Acrobatic Show* from the Song Dynasty. In the picture, the acrobatic performer sings and beats the drum at the same time, attracting two children.

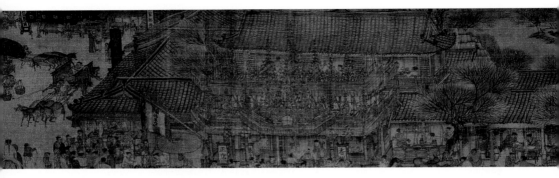

Scroll of *Along the River During the Qingming Festival*, by Zhang Zeduan of the Song Dynasty. This is a vivid depiction of the bustling capital city Bianliang of the Northern Song Dynasty, showing a theatre next to the street in the left of the picture.

A Silk painting of Song *zaju*, in which two actresses play male roles, a popular theatrical convention during the Song Dynasty.

oriented entertainment and arts industries converged and fierce market competition put considerable pressure on individual theatre troupes, which responded by working to increase performance standards.

Buddhism, which emerged in China during the Eastern Han Dynasty (25–220), was also a catalyst for the prosperity of the story-telling theatre which characterized the Tang and Song dynasties. A style called *bianwen* emerged in Buddhist temples, where Suttantikas (Buddhist chanters) encouraged the monks to translate scriptures into vernacular prose and then into songs. The monks' *bianwen* allowed them to preach through popular forms and became a kind of mass entertainment.

From *bianwen*, *zhu gongdiao* was created. *Zhu Gongdiao Romance of the West Chamber* (*Xi Xiang Ji Zhu Gongdiao*) by Dong Jieyuan, was the best work of *zhu gongdiao* of its time (it was later adapted into the classic play *Romance of the West Chamber*

A brick carving of Jin *zaju* at a tomb in Jishan, Shanxi province, vividly describes the postures and expression of *zaju* characters.

(*Xi Xiang Ji*), one of the most famous plays in the history of Chinese theatre). In the play, a young man on his way to sit the imperial examinations meets a beautiful woman. They fall in love at first sight and secretly get engaged, but are then forced to separate under pressure from their families. When the man comes first in the final examination, he wins his lover back. Meeting, loving, parting and reunion were the basic elements of this dramatic form. *Zhu Gongdiao Romance of the West Chamber* also included fourteen different *gongdiao* and about 150 basic melodies making it one of the many large-scale musical works which emerged during the Sui and Tang dynasties. However, as narratives became more complex, a more varied musical pattern was required. *Zhu gongdiao* began to draw on Tang and Song folk music and Song *ci* poetry for inspiration.

Gongdiao
Gongdiao is a term used in ancient Chinese theatre that refers to various musical modes, which then sets a dramatic tune. The order of twelve temperaments with seven tunes, including *gong*, *shang*, *jiao*, *zhi*, *yu*, *biangong* and *bianzhi* was the basic order followed in all dynasties. The musical mode dominated by the *gong* temperament is called *gong*, otherwise, it was *diao*. Seven tunes accompanied by twelve temperaments could create twelve *gong* and seventy-two *diao*, forging eighty-four *gongdiao*.

Towering Peaks: Song *Xiwen* and Yuan *Zaju*

Southern *Xiwen* during the Song Dynasty

During the late Southern Song Dynasty (1127–1279), a new kind of play emerged which had a set length and a full narrative, where actors performed through speech and singing. This sophisticated style emerged in Wenzhou and flourished in the southern area around the Yangtze River and was known as "southern tune *xiwen*" or simply referred to as *xiwen*.

The earliest complete book of *xiwen* scripts was found in 1920 in a small antique shop in London by the scholar Ye Gongchuo. It includes works such as *The No.1 Scholar Zhang Xie* (*Zhang Xie Zhuang Yuan*), *The Butcher* (*Xiao Sun Tu*) and *An Official's Son Opts for the Wrong Career* (*Huan Men Zi Di Cuo Li Shen*).

The No.1 Scholar Zhang Xie was written by scholars in the Jiushan Club in Wenzhou. *Xiwen* performances were very popular in Wenzhou and literary societies were common. The Jiushan Club, a professional group of script writers, took an active role in local affairs so that when, in one case, a corrupt monk named Zu Jie was being protected by local officials, club members immediately compiled a *xiwen* script based on the monk's misdemeanors and performed the play in public. The play aroused the anger of the local population, forcing the government to punish the monk. This incident demonstrates the important role that theatre played in society during the Southern Song Dynasty.

The scholars of the Jiushan Club came from the lower and middle classes. Having been well trained in poetry writing from early childhood, their script-writing skills were developed through regular contact with popular music and dance artists. Their scripts, such as *The No.1 Scholar Zhang Xie*, laid the literary foundations for Chinese folk theatre, which from that time onwards began to develop large-scale theatrical performances.

The No.1 Scholar Zhang Xie tells the story of Zhang who, on his way to the imperial examination, is accosted by bandits on Wuji Mountain. Robbed and seriously wounded, he flees to a nearby temple where he encounters a poor maiden who earns a living by weaving cotton cloth. The two marry and vow to spend their remaining years together. Two months after their marriage, Zhang recovers and decides to continue his journey to Beijing to take the exams. Since he is penniless and cannot afford the long journey, his wife sells her hair to cover his traveling expenses. Zhang goes to the capital and comes first in the examination. His success attracts the attention of Wang Jinhua, the daughter of Prime Minister Wang Deyong. However, Zhang rejects Wang Jinhua, who dies of a broken heart. Meanwhile, Zhang's wife has followed Zhang to Beijing after learning of his success. The newly elevated Zhang looks down on her for her humble origins and drives her out of the imperial building. Later, Zhang is assigned an office outside of Beijing and on his way there he passes through Wuji Mountain and meets his wife, who begs him to take her back. Zhang tries to kill her with his sword and she is seriously injured falling off a cliff.

The No. 1 Scholar Zhang Xie.

At the same time, Prime Minister Wang Deyong asks to become Zhang's supervisor. On his way to take this position, he saves Zhang's wounded wife and adopts her as his daughter. Zhang, attempting to make amends for his earlier rejection of Wang's daughter Wang Jinhua, asks to marry this daughter. In the bridal chamber, Zhang recognizes the wife he abandoned and is ashamed. She refuses to marry him, but at last, persuaded by Wang, the two overcome their differences and marry.

The No.1 Scholar Zhang Xie is an exciting story with a winding, complicated plot. The play focuses on the portrayal of poor, weak women, while high ranking officials are heavily criticized. The authors' moral and political standpoint was clear, and it was this didactic element which set the tone for the plays of this era.

Xiwen spread widely during the Southern Song Dynasty through works such as *The Chaste Woman Zhao and Cai Erlang* (*Zhao Zhen Nü Cai Er Lang*) and *Wang Kui Betrays Gui-Ying* (*Wang Kui Fu Gui Ying*). Their themes were similar to *The No.1 Scholar Zhang Xie*, portraying men who rise to fortune and subsequently betray their original lovers. The poor and disadvantaged women in these plays were always portrayed more sympathetically than the men and thus these plays appealed to ordinary people because of the audacity they showed in rewarding virtue and punishing vice.

That *xiwen* plays such as *The No.1 Scholar Zhang Xie* were able to emerge during the Song Dynasty is in some senses astonishing, given that during this period the Song were repeatedly being defeated in their wars with the Liao (907–1125) and Jin. Eventually the Song migrated to the south and the Jin took the north, resulting in a 150-year-long division between the north and south of China. It was in the capital of the Southern Song Dynasty, Lin'an (present-day Hangzhou), that theatrical entertainments flourished.

The office in charge of music at the imperial court alternated, according to its political leanings, between founding and abolishing

Dramatic roles fall into five categories: *sheng* (a male lead), *dan* (a female lead), *jing* (a supporting male lead), *chou* (the jester) and *mo* (a male role). These roles can be further divided according to gender, age and characteristics. This photo shows a *Laosheng* (an old male lead) and a *Huadan* (a young female lead).

theatrical projects. As a result, a large group of artists, originally trained at the court but often no longer required there, began to participate in public performances, raising performance standards and intensifying competition between theatrical troupes. *Xiwen* was the product of the more ornate styles these performers brought with them.

The No.1 Scholar Zhang Xie departed from earlier forms of theatre that simplistically combined speech with song—it was a fully-fledged theatrical form. It was a typical prosopopeia in genre and narrative method. It also possessed a complete musical structure, with "southern tune" at its centre.

It is true that *xiwen*, including *The No.1 Scholar Zhang Xie*, was closely related to the basic sung and spoken performances of *bianwen* and *zhu gongdiao* of the Tang and Song dynasties whose stories, themes and characters were well known to audiences.

However, *xiwen* transformed the generic conventions of these earlier forms. While *bianwen* and *zhu gongdiao* were narratives, *xiwen* was prosopopeia. Theatre thus became a form separate from the art of singing and story-telling. In the latter form, one or two narrators told the story using the third person form of speech. Conversely, actors in *xiwen* theatre all played character roles so that the story was told through the first person. With the same storylines and the same characters, but with different means of expression, theatre became clearly distinct from other forms of performance.

The script of *The No.1 Scholar Zhang Xie*, bears the traces of this change from *zhu gongdiao* to *xiwen*. For example the opening scenes are similar to *zhu gongdiao*; an actor-narrator urges the audience to be quiet then relates how the play came into being and how it was adapted from the original *zhu gongdiao* work *The Biography of No. 1 Scholar Zhang Xie* (*Zhang Xie Zhuang Yuan Zhuan*).

In *xiwen* plays, actors played stock dramatic characters. *The No.1 Scholar Zhang Xie* included a *sheng* (a male lead), *dan* (a female lead), *jing* (a supporting male lead), *chou* (the jester) and *mo* (a male role). Sometimes these roles would be supplemented by *wai* (an additional role). In *The No.1 Scholar Zhang Xie*, a *sheng* played the role of Zhang, while the poor maiden was played by the *dan*. However, actors were not confined to one character and often took on two or three character roles. In *The No.1 Scholar Zhang Xie*, *mo*, *jing* and *chou* all appear frequently, taking part in multiple scenes. In most plays *jing* and *chou* were comic parts, the descendents of *canjun* and *canghu* from Canjun Opera. *Mo* was a character-narrator, who, from time to time, would jump out of the narrative of the play to introduce an event or comment on the action.

From the Song Dynasty onwards, when actors performed on stages and learned their parts from scripts, character roles where indicated in the script by their stock names, for example *sheng* or *dan*, rather than character names such as Zhang Xie or the poor maiden. This demonstrates how Chinese theatre scripts were primarily aids for stage actors, rather than texts for reading or studying. The scripts gave the actors indications about who was next to go on stage, the order of action and the emotional tone of the scene, rather than story or character information.

The No.1 Scholar Zhang Xie is a piece of physical theatre. A typical example of the use of physical techniques is when Zhang is seriously injured by bandits and escapes to a nearby temple. The setting is changed by *jing, mo* and *chou*, who in this piece play the Mountain God, the judge and the clown. When Zhang enters the temple, *jing* orders *mo* and *chou* to change into two temple doors. As Zhang pushes the door, therefore, what he actually pushes is *mo* and *chou*. Since Zhang is badly wounded, he has to lean against the door when it is closed, and leans on *chou*. Later, when the poor maiden returns to the temple, she has to knock at the same door and *chou*, impersonating the door, makes the sound of her knocking. When the poor maiden moves to knock, *chou* even says, "you could also knock on the other door." On the wedding day, *mo* takes the role of Uncle

Stock characters
The stock characters in traditional Chinese opera were formed from the division of acting responsibilities in early theatrical troupes and originated in two-role Canjun Operas. Actors each performed a particular stock character such as *sheng, dan, jing, chou,* or *mo*. However as plots became more complex, it was often the case that two or more of the same stock characters were required on stage at the same time and so troupes had to expand. Similar stock characters in theatre companies were placed in a hierarchy. For example, when two *dan* were needed for one production, perhaps to play a mistress and a maid servant, the more important role of the mistress would be played by the leading first *dan*, and the supporting role by the second *dan*.

A male *chou* and a female *chou*.

Li, while *jing* is Aunt *Li*, and *chou* the waiter. However, at the wedding reception, *chou* gets down on all fours to serve as a dinner table. When Zhang Xie, the poor maiden, Uncle Zhang and Aunt Li drink the wine, the table begins to sing: "I bow from the waist to serve you, so may you be so kind as to offer with me some wine to drink?"

Such performances, which no doubt teased audiences, encapsulate the typical style of staged Chinese theatre at this time and such physical theatre has, from its inception during the Song Dynasty, been fundamental to the development of Chinese theatre.

In the twentieth century, Chinese theatrical scholars named this theatrical form *xiqu*. *Xiqu* carries the legacy of all of the simple folk plays of the past thousand years of Chinese theatre.

The Prosperity of Yuan *Zaju*

The thirteenth century saw the destruction of the Southern Song Dynasty by the Mongols, which lead to the establishment of a unified Yuan Dynasty. The Mongols ruled China, especially the south, with an iron hand. Yet despite this period of repression, it was during this time that some of the most important developments in the history of Chinese theatre took place.

During the Yuan Dynasty, *zaju* was the predominant theatrical form in prosperous cities such as Kaifeng, Luoyang and Lin'an. It was performed by courtesans who were also singers for the amusement of officials of the court or local government. The courtesans were permitted to put on some public performances which, bolstered by traveling theatrical troupes, made *zaju* the mainstream dramatic form of the period.

Zaju spread throughout the country to rural areas. Its prosperity was partially enabled by scholars who, keen to avoid the politics of the court instead interacted with artists and performers from the lower social classes and wrote scripts for them.

Yuan *zaju* was also known as "northern tune" *zaju*, to distinguish it from southern tune *xiwen*. There were sharp differences in the musical performances of the south and north during the Song and Yuan dynasties. Although southern tune *xiwen* appeared before northern tune *zaju*, the latter was a distinct, separate musical system which developed independently. Nor did Yuan *zaju* influence Song Jin *zaju*. Although both forms have the same name, Song Jin *zaju* was a small-scale comic form, where music was incidental and narratives incomplete. These stylistic qualities were, of course, present in Yuan *zaju*, but only as interludes which provided actors with a break, and allowed audiences to take in the implications of the main acts.

Both *zaju* and *xiwen* were influenced by song and dance forms such as *zhu gongdiao*. A comparison between the surviving fragments of *zhu gongdiao* and Yuan *zaju* plays with similar themes, shows that Yuan *zaju* reproduced the conventions of *zhu gongdiao* in its set melodic lines, the alternation between speaking and singing, its large-scale productions and comprehensive story telling.

A mural at Guangsheng Temple in Hongtong County, Shanxi Province depicting the performance of Yuan *zaju*.

A painting from the Baoning Temple in Youyu County, Shanxi Province, depicting a traveling theatrical troupe of the Yuan Dynasty with their musical instruments.

Yuan *zaju* typically has four *zhe* (acts), preceded by a *xiezi* (an introduction or prologue). The four *zhe* are four set musical pieces, each based on a different *gongdiao*. Each *gongdiao* has several fixed *qupai* (melodies) which are arranged in set patterns. Each set piece has a common introductory melody, which in *zheng gongdiao* is usually *duan zhenghao*, and in *xianlü gong* is *dian jiangchun*. The name of the piece is derived from a combination of its first melody with the type of gongdiao it is. So *"xianlu · dian jiangchun,"* for example, is the name of a piece which adopts *xianlu* as its *gongdiao* and *dian jiangchun* as its first melody. Each piece also has a fixed ending, a *shawei* or *shousha*. Sometimes, a piece ends with several *shawei*, arranged in reverse order. The set musical pieces of Yuan *zaju* are thus well structured from their set introductions and first melodies to their set *shawei* or epilogues. *Xiezi* often comes before the four *zhe*, operating as a prelude by describing the plot and characters. However there are exceptions to this rule; in *Tears on the Blue Gown* (*Qing Shan Lei*) the *xiezi* occurs between the first and second *zhe* and in *Orphan of Zhao* (*Zhao Shi Gu Er*), the *xiezi* comes before by a short fifth *zhe*, which is effectively the end of the play.

In Yuan *zaju* the style of *qiang* (the melody) and *ban* (the rhythm) vary. Various rhythms within the same mode can be used to express feelings, narrate events and create distinctive theatrical atmospheres. When a set musical group is based on the same mode, the lines should use the same rhyme. As a general rule in

Yuan *zaju*, there are usually four pieces of music in each of the four *zhe*, with the lines employing four different feet. That general rule with four rhymes in four musical sets with a variety of lines and tunes to display the ups and downs of the language styles in the entire theatre suggests that the dramatists and players were versatile enough to utilize various means to strengthen dramatic effect.

As with *xiwen*, Yuan *zaju* had strict rules concerning dramatic roles, but *zaju* focused on the principal male and female characters. Therefore, there are two types of performance, one with a male main role and one with a female main role. The singing courtesans always played the leading role, whether the character was a man or a woman. Records from Yuan brothels show that several girls excelled at playing male characters, whilst others were talented at acting both male and female roles. The singing girls in brothels managed by the government formed the main performance groups of the time, and a convention developed where a particular well-known singing girl would be given center stage, so that the entire opera would focus on her performance. This happens in Ma Zhiyuan's *Autumn in the Han Palace* (*Han Gong Qiu*) and in the anonymously written *Zhang Yi's Indifference to Su Qin* (*Dong Su Qin*). The two plays both focus on male characters and from beginning to end are performed exclusively by male actors. The same thing happens in Guan Hanqing's *Official Qian Treats Lady Xie Wisely* (*Qian Da Yin Zhi Chong Xie Tian Xiang*), but in these plays the central character is female/played by a female actress. In the opera *Xue Rengui*, the main character Xue is played by a supporting actor, not the main singer, although the story develops around him. As Yuan *zaju* has only one main performer the general rule is that the main performer should play the role that requires singing and not necessarily the part of the hero. For example, Shang Zhongxian's *Liu Yi Sending Love Signal in Dongting Lake* (*Dong Ting Hu Liu Yi Chuan Shu*) is female-oriented theatre. The main female performer plays the heroine in the introduction, and in the first, third and fourth *zhe*, but in the second *zhe* she plays the goddess who is in charge of lightning. In *Xue Rengui* a male performer plays the part of the official in arms, Lord Cai, in the first *zhe*, the peer who spent his childhood with Xue in the third, while in the second and fourth he plays the role of Xue's father.

As *zaju* developed and audiences grew larger, theatrical troupes began to expand and the traditional stock character roles started to divide. The role of *dan* (the female lead) gradually subdivided into the female lead, female supporting actor, young female, old female and comic female. The *mo* (male lead) divided into male lead, the supporting male, young male and treacherous male.

The large number of Yuan *zaju* plays is a remarkable achievement. The *Register of Ghosts* (*Lu Gui Bu*) compiled by Zhong Sicheng (1279–1360) lists 152 *zaju* playwrights and over 450 works. Jia Zhongming (1343–1422) added a further 71 playwrights and 156 works during the transition between the Yuan and Ming dynasties. During the Ming Dynasty Zang Fanxun (1550–1620) compiled the *Selection of Yuan Theatre* (*Yuan Qu Xuan*), in which he identified 94 different kinds of Yuan *zaju* and 6 *zaju* of the early Ming Dynasty. His contemporary, Sui Shusen, contributed 62 theatrical works of the Yuan and early Ming dynasties to the compilation, whose transcripts survive to this day.

Yuan *zaju* also contributed to Chinese literary culture. The most famous examples of ancient Chinese literature are *Tangshi, Songci* and *Yuanqu* (poems from the Tang Dynasty, *ci* poetry from the Song and *zaju* from the Yuan). *Yuanqu* is the name given for *sanqu* (a type of verse with tonal patterns modeled on tunes drawn from folk music). Yuan *zaju* employs both verse and prose, integrating the verse with the music in its narratives, demonstrating playwrights' tremendous ability in mastering complicated writing forms which synchronize with the music.

The themes of Yuan *zaju* may be divided into twelve broad categories; the mystical world, the life of hermits, officialdom, martyrs, faithfulness to family, punishing the treacherous, the exiled subject and orphan heir, the uprising of the oppressed classes, romance, gathering and departure, singing girls and courtesans, and Buddha and spirit.

The most well-known dramatists were Guan Hanqing, Wang Shifu, Ma Zhiyuan and Bai Pu.

Wang Shifu was born sometime in the late thirteenth century or early fourteenth century, but little is known about his life, other than that he frequently visited brothels (a fact which becomes evident from hints in his poetry).He wrote thirteen plays, among them *A Tumbledown Cave* (*Lü Meng Zheng Feng Xue Po Yao Ji*) and his masterpiece *Romance of the Western Chamber* (*Xi Xiang Ji*).

Romance of the Western Chamber is based on *Zhu Gongdiao of Romance of the Western Chamber*, and took inspiration from the Tang Dynasty poet Yuan Zhen's *Story of Yingying* (*Ying Ying Zhuan*). It also drew on the *guzici Butterfly and Flowers*.

Romance of the Western Chamber tells the story of the daughter of Premier Cui during the Tang Dynasty and the struggles which she and her mother face in taking Premier Cui's coffin back home for burial. On their journey, the women stop at the famous Pujiu Temple. Zhang Junrui, on his way to the imperial examination, happens to pass by and encounters the young Lady Cui (Yingying) by chance in the Buddha hall. Fixated by her beauty, he decides to go to the temple in the hope of meeting her again. Meanwhile, a gang led by Sun Feihu hears of Yingying's breathtaking beauty and besieges the temple, intending to capture her. Yingying's mother pronounces that whoever is able to rescue them can have her daughter's hand in

Guzici
Guzici is a type of spoken performance popular during the Song Dynasty. It is composed of both prose and verse, the latter being comprised of ten stanzas. Early *guzici* was sung repeatedly to the same tune, without advancing the narrative. However, Zhao Lingzhi's *Butterfly and Flowers* is a kind of *guzici* which tells the story of two young lovers, through one prose speech and a stanza of singing. The singing part uses the same lines repeated twelve times.

An illustration of *Romance of the West Chamber*. In the picture the heroine, Cui Yingying is reading a letter from her beloved, while her maid Hongniang peeps from behind a screen.

marriage. Zhang writes to an old friend and persuades him to send forces to frighten the gang away. However, having been rescued, old Lady Cui goes back on her word and the frustrated Zhang falls ill. Yingying, who likes Zhang, feels guilty about her mother's behavior. The two begin an affair in secret. A month later, old Lady Cui notices something between them and asks Yingying's servant what is going on. The maid, Hongniang, feels compelled to tell the truth and persuades old Lady Cui to allow their marriage. Lady Cui declares that the high status of the Cui family requires that Zhang attempt the imperial examination and win an official position before marrying Yingying. Zhang and Yingying are separated, but Yingying's spirit stays with Zhang all the way to the examination. Zhang passes the exam and the tale ends happily with their reunion.

The Kunqu Opera *Romance of the West Chamber* performed by the Northern Kunqu Opera Theatre.

This play's portrayal of the love between two young people won much praise. Wang's ability to represent the emotions is impressive. When he writes about how Zhang and Yingying could not be together despite their close proximity to each other, he does so through the song of the clever maid Hongniang:

> *She languishes as the handsome man wrinkles his forehead,*
> *His beauty not the same as before, the waist slimmer and the clothes looser,*
> *One drowsy without any attention to his books,*
> *One absent-minded unable to do her embroidery;*
> *One playing melancholic tunes on the instrument,*
> *One, heartbroken, writing lines on the paper with little expectation;*
> *The same lovesickness for both.*

When saying goodbye to Zhang, Yingying's singing part is rich with images of the colors of nature, which she evokes to alleviate her sadness at their parting. It quickly became a classic literary stanza:

> *With clouds the sky turns grey,*
> *over yellow-blow-paved way*
> *How bitter blows the western breeze!*
> *From north to south fly the wild geese.*
> *Why like a wine-flushed face, is the frosted forest red?*
> *It is dyed with the tears parting lovers shed.*
> *So late we met, so soon we part; the long willow branch cannot tie the rein, wishing the sun was fixed on the branch of time without flying; the horse runs fast in front, while the carriage follows after; without talking openly we pretended to avoid suspicion, with our love public, parting comes so soon. As soon as I heard the word leaving spoken, my golden armbands grew loose. From far away I had only to see the pavilion and my jade white flesh wasted away. Can any one understand my complaint?*

The complex changes of emotions felt by the young lovers are portrayed from the beginning of the play when Zhang cannot stop thinking of Yingying, whilst by the departure scene it is Yingying who demonstrates her tender feelings by singing,

> With views of the mountains all around us, the whip echoes in the sunset. Love, more than anything in the world, occupies my mind; but how can the small carriage carry it? I will write to you as often as possible, and you need not swear that you won't return without success. There is just one thing of which you should think; that no matter how far away you are, it will never be anything like here.

The differences between the desires of Yingying and Zhang indicate the setbacks they will face on their road to marriage. Their marriage is not only prevented by family; more dramatically, it is Yingying's thirst for love, yet hesitation in accepting the love of Zhang, which adds a much more thought-provoking element to the tale.

Great writers are often adept at exposing the hidden depths of human nature. The play's happy ending demonstrates that it is human nature which ultimately wins through over and above the different beliefs of the two generations.

Wang's *Romance of Western Chamber* differs from other Yuan *zaju* in being performed in twenty scenes contained in five acts, rather than the usual four acts. There is some suspicion as to whether the fifth act was actually written by Wang, since the majority of the action takes place in the first four. Nonetheless, Wang's *Romance of Western Chamber* has been performed on stage countless times since its inception.

Ma Zhiyuan is another significant playwright from the Yuan Dynasty and his well-received *Autumn in the Han Palace (Han Gong Qiu)* is considered to be the best example of Yuan theatre.

An illustration of *Autumn in the Han Palace*. It shows Wang Zhaojun leaving for the frontier in pursuit of peace.

The play focuses on the tragic love between Emperor Yuandi of the Han Dynasty and Wang Zhaojun, the most beautiful lady of the time. Despite being born into an ordinary family, Zhaojun is selected as a possible wife for the emperor and is invited to the palace. However, she refuses to bribe the imperial painter Mao Yanshou, who is responsible for painting images of the female suitors. As a result, Mao makes Zhaojun look ugly so she misses the opportunity for an audience with the emperor. However, Zhaojun can play the pipa (a four-stringed Chinese lute) very well and one day the emperor is attracted by the sound of her pipa and calls her in. He sees Zhaojun's great beauty and she becomes his favorite. Mao's corruption is discovered, and the painter flees to the Fan tribe, where he convinces the tribe's leader to ask for Wang Zhaojun's hand in marriage, and to threaten war if his request is not granted. Unable to defend the empire against the tribe, the emperor is forced to give up Zhaojun. Without her he is lonely and pines for his absent beauty.

After sending Zhaojun to the Fan tribe, the emperor's misery is vividly described by Ma Zhiyuan:

> *Facing the wild grasses, people carrying spears, horses loading essentials, carriages taking army provisions, paddocks being enclosed,*

she bid farewell to her lord, and I too had to say goodbye. After she was given to the wild world outside I went back to the palace. Back to the palace, through gate after gate, along the corridors, to the bedroom. On this lonely and cold evening, here with the green window screen, I cannot stop missing her, my lady! Oh, my tears roll down my cheeks. This vision of my lady will stay with me tonight.

The play does not end happily with the loving days the hero and heroine spend together, but with the emperor's suffering and longing for Zhaojun after their separation. Yet he not only mourns for his lost love but for the weakness of his kingdom and his humiliation at having to send his concubine in order to keep the peace, rather than face losing a war.

Orphan of Zhao (*Zhao Shi Gu Er*) by Ji Junxiang, another influential play from the Yuan Dynasty, takes place during the Spring and Autumn Period and tells the tale of warriors who make great sacrifices to protect the orphan heir of a city state. It focuses on an old man's humiliation and efforts to raise the child, which he endures so that he might eventually take revenge.

Orphan of Zhao was well received and in 1731 the French priest Joseph Ma translated the play into French. In 1775 Voltaire re-translated it, and it became the play *Chinese Orphan*. Along with *The Chalk Circle* (*Hui Lan Ji*), *Orphan of Zhao* is an example of a Chinese play which has successfully been adapted for performance in the Western world.

The Peking Opera *Orphan of Zhao*.

The Shaoxing Opera version of *Orphan of Zhao* performed by the Shanghai Yue Opera Troupe.

Guan Hanqing's Remarkable Achievement

There are many famous writers from the Yuan Dynasty, but Guan Hanqing was without doubt the most talented. We do not know much about his life, other than that he lived during the thirteenth century, at the time of the transition from the Jin to the Yuan Dynasty. It is said that he may have been a doctor in the capital city or that he once he worked as a court physician.

Despite experiencing difficulties in his life, he bore them with good humour, declaring "I am the leader of both honorable men and prodigals" and "I am a genuine bronze bean that cannot be boiled into pieces or thoroughly stewed, beaten flat or cracked by frying."

His important role in Yuan theatre is evident from the title he was given: "the leader of *liyuan*, the composers and the dramatists," the *liyuan* being a type of theatre where plays were performed. Guan Hanqing wrote more than sixty plays, eighteen of which remain as complete scripts. *The Injustice to Dou E* (*Dou E Yuan*), *Preparing a Fish for the Mid-Autumn Festival* (*Wang Jiang Ting Zhong Qiu Qie*

Kuai), *Zhao Pan'er Rescues her Sisters through Cunning* (*Zhao Pan Er Feng Yue Jiu Feng Chen*), *The Moon-Prayer Pavilion* (*Gui Yuan Jia Ren Bai Yue Ting*), *Judge Bao Wisely has Lu Beheaded* (*Bao Dai Zhi Zhi Zhan Lu Zhai Lang*), and *Lord Guan Goes to the Feast* (*Guan Da Wang Du Fu Dan Dao Hui*) are all fantastic examples.

In *The Injustice to Dou E*, the heroine, Dou E, is a young widow who marries into the Cai family when her father goes for the imperial examination. Her husband dies young and she goes to live with her old and weak mother-in-law, who makes a living as a money

A portrait of Guan Hanqing.

lender. The evil Doctor Sai intends to cancel his debts by killing the old woman when she goes to collect her payment. A father and son named Zhang pass by and save her life. The old Lady Cai invites them to her house to thank them.

However, the father and son then try to force Dou E and her mother-in-law into marrying them. Dou E refuses their offer. The young Zhang tries to poison Lady Cai but his father drinks the poisoned soup instead and dies. The young Zhang brings a false charge against Lady Cai for poisoning his father.

Without any solid evidence, the officials torture Lady Cai and Dou E is forced to admit to the false charge herself, in order to save her mother-in-law from being tortured. As a result, Dou E is sentenced to death. At the execution ground, she appeals to heaven as she makes three pledges: That her blood will stain the white ground, that it will snow in June, and that there will be a three year drought. After her death, one by one each of her predictions comes true. Meanwhile, her father, Dou Tianzhang, has successfully completed the exam and won the trust of the court. He is appointed as an inspector of the different regions. When he arrives in Chuzhou, which has been suffering from a three-year drought, he dreams of his daughter (who he has not seen for sixteen years)

The Shaanxi Opera *The Injustice to Dou E*. In the photograph, the falsely accused Dou E is being taken to the execution ground.

pouring out her grievances. Dou Tianzhang investigates the case and punishes the real murderer and the corrupt officials. Although Dou E finally receives justice, she cannot return from the dead.

As in many of Guan's works, the play focuses on the grievances of a vulnerable woman. Guan was sympathetic to poor, helpless women of the lower classes and in Dou E he creates an archetypal downtrodden character. She was ill treated in the court, being beaten twice. As she said "A brief respite, only to stir, and swoon again. Another strike, a stream of blood, a strip of skin." When about to be executed, Guan writes lines for Dou E which boldly proclaim her grievances:

> There is no reason for you to break the law with this false charge. In a rather short time, I am sentenced to death, how can I bear the injustice without any complaint? There is the sun and the moon for the day and night, and there is a god who is in control of life and

The Puzhou Clapper Opera *The Injustice to Dou E.* In this scene Dou E is reunited with her long-lost father.

death. God should be capable of telling right from wrong, but now vice is being rewarded and virtue is being punished. Oh, God of Heaven and Earth, how you bully the weak and fear the strong. God of Earth, you cannot tell right from wrong, and God of Heaven, you reward vice and punish virtue. How could that be your duty? You leave me with tears rolling...

In the fourth act, the spirit of Dou E appears on the stage, singing "every day I wait with tears at the place that was my hometown, eagerly awaiting the murderer. I walk slowly in darkness, float in the hurricane, am lost in the fog and cloud."

Guan not only portrays the hardship of this fragile women's life, but also emphasizes the heroine's kindheartedness. Dou E admits to the false charge out of a sense of family loyalty to her mother-in-law, sacrificing herself so that her mother-in-law might not be tortured.

When facing execution, her only request is to take a back way to the execution ground, sparing her mother-in-law the sight of her on her way to be executed. When her father finally delivers justice, her

The Hebei Clapper Opera *The Injustice to Dou E.* In the picture, the gracefully floating opera-water sleeve vividly shows the grievance of Dou E, successfully achieving a fantastic stage effect.

only wish is that her father might take care of her mother-in-law. At all times Dou E thinks of her mother-in-law's needs before her own.

The play drew on the story of *The Daughter-in-law in the East China Sea (Dong Hai Xiao Fu)*, where the heroine's actions are rooted in her fidelity to her family, even though her elder is not a blood relative, a fact which makes her kindness all the more noble.

The Injustice to Dou E demonstrates Guan's mastery of expression. For example, Doctor Sai says "In medicine there is room to change one's mind, for prescriptions there is always the old tert; there's no way of bringing the dead to life, the living can always be doctored to death." Tao Wu, the fatuous official, fell to the ground on his knees after the accused was on his knees. Tao explained to his servant, who did not understand, "you should know that the people who came to bring a lawsuit are the bread and meal to me." When conducting the trial, he only knows how to use torture, saying "men are worthless creatures, they never confess without any beating. Servant, choose a large staff and keep on beating."

The characters are played through *jing* roles, which use exaggeration and irony to comic effect. The most outstanding feature of Guan's work is that he was able to apply the strict set rhythms of the form to the language of the common people, which he uses throughout the play.

From this point onwards, playwrights tended to select materials closer to the tastes of the lower classes and familiar to the public, creating plays which appealed to thousands of people. Their skillful employment of folkloric songs and poetry has ensured that the idioms and musical tones of the Song and Yuan Dynasties continue to flourish in Chinese theatre.

Refinement and Elegance: *Chuanqi* of the Ming and Qing Dynasties and Kunqu Opera

Scholars Reinvent *Xiwen*

As Yuan *zaju* shifted its creative hub from the north to the south it did not take long for Wenzhou, along with neighboring Lin'an, the ancient capital of the Southern Song Dynasty, to become China's most important opera centers for what were now fully-fledged operative performances.

Xiwen re-emerged during the late Yuan and early Ming dynasties in the south of China in reaction to the dominance of northern *zaju*. In order to compete with northern *zaju* and its literary masters, *xiwen* works became more complex. One successful example of this modification was written by the playwright Gao Ming, elevating southern *xiwen* from the realm of folklore through plays such as *Story of the Pipa (Pi Pa Ji)*, so that it gradually replaced northern *zaju*, ushering in a new era of Chinese opera.

Gao Ming was born in the early fourteenth century and lived until the late Yuan or early Ming Dynasty. At the age of forty, Gao was serving as a minor official but he soon retired, moving to the town of Lishe in the east of Ningbo. It was here that Gao wrote his great work *Story of the Pipa*. It is believed that in order to write the play, he worked and slept in a small building for the three years that it took him to finish the work.

Story of the Pipa is about the joys and sorrows of Zhao Wuniang and Cai Bojie. The plot drew on an earlier *xiwen* work of the Song Dynasty where Cai Bojie is separated from his love, Zhao, when he leaves for the capital in search of an official position. However, once his efforts have met with success, he abandons his family. He is eventually killed by being struck by lightning. The story delved deeply into ethics and common values, focusing on the tragic life of Zhao Wuniang.

Southern *xiwen* during the Song and Yuan dynasties was considered to be a low art form which, despite portraying the differences between love and hate, lacked a literary quality.

Gao Ming rewrote the story, keeping the original content and sympathetic character of Zhao Wuniang, but placing the emphasis on Cai Bojie through an in-depth exploration of Cai's psychological states. In Gao Ming's version, it is the three disobediences of Cai Bojie which take center stage.

Story of the Pipa begins with the emergence of Cai Bojie as a dutiful son. He initially refuses the officials who want to recruit him, for the sake of his parents. However his father reprimands him, telling him to value his prospects rather than relying on family love and affection. Reluctant to leave home, Cai Bojie bids farewell to his parents and his wife and leaves for the capital to take part in the imperial examinations. He wins first place in the exams, but difficulties quickly ensue. The emperor wants to oversee the wedding ceremony of the daughter of a senior adviser named Niu, and orders Cai Bojie to marry her. Cai Bojie puts forward many excuses to avoid the marriage but to no avail. Finally, he asks to see the emperor and explains that he cannot serve as an official but must return home to look after his parents. However, the senior advisor uses his influence at court to cover up the fact that Cai Bojie has a wife and elderly parents. He urges the emperor to refuse his request, leaving Cai Bojie's wife and parents to suffer.

Refusing the examination, marriage, and an official rank, are Cai's three disobediences which see him transformed from the ambitious, callous man of the first version of the play into a helpless character who, despite coming first in the imperial examination, is eager to go home. Forced to stay at Niu's house, he misses his parents and virtuous wife and becomes depressed. He sings: "The old ties have been broken, but I am not accustomed to the new ones. It is impossible to have the old ties again, but I will fight hard to rid myself of the new ones. I have tried, but again and again I am thwarted by officials."

Story of the Pipa highlights Cai Bojie's anxiety, but also his virtue.

The Kunqu Opera *Story of the Pipa*, performed by the Jiangsu Suzhou Kunqu Troupe. In this scene Cai Bojie and Miss Niu get married.

Where the original leading character in the story had been Zhao Wuniang, Gao Ming made Cai Bojie the hero of his play, whilst maintaining the kindness and virtuousness of Zhao.

Story of the Pipa's plot consists of two parallel storylines set in two different locations.

The story uses the symbol of the lotus, moon and other scenarios to express the deep concern and longing of Cai Bojie. Zhao's hardships are portrayed through her actions; she eats chaff and shaves off her hair to become a nun. Zhao eats chaff and preserved vegetables so that her in-laws might eat the remaining grain, but her action is given another significance:

> *Vomiting is painful and fills me with tears. Oh, chaff! You were milled and screened and just like my own pains, you have experienced great hardships. A bitter person eats bitter food, we are two kinds of bitterness meeting, both hard to swallow.*
>
> *Chaff and rice are mutually dependent, but they are separated by winnowing. One is mean and the other is noble, just like my husband*

*and I, having no chance to meet again. My husband, you are rice. You are
gone, but I cannot look for you. I am the chaff but how can I save others
from hunger with chaff? How can I serve my in-laws with good food?*

Gao Ming uses the well-known metaphor of chaff, evoking the
notion of a husk, in his depiction of the poor wife. Cai's parents die
from sadness, one after the other. With no money, Zhao sells her
hair to pay for their burials.

In traditional Chinese culture, hair is a symbol of the first formal
marriage between a man and a woman. When Zhao sells her hair,
therefore, this is a deeply meaningful moment. She even uses her
clothes to carry soil to erect a tomb for her parents-in-law. She goes to
the capital carrying a pipa and with help from Ms Niu, the couple
are finally reunited. Ms Niu persuades her father to allow Cai Bojie
to resign from his official post and return to his hometown to offer
a sacrifice to his parents.

The Kunqu Opera *Story of the Pipa*, performed by the Jiangsu Suzhou Kunqu Troupe. In this
scene Zhao Wuniang eats chaff of the remaining grain in front of her in-laws, invoking their pity.

The story ends with Cai Bojie taking his two wives to sweep his parents' tombs.

The greatness of *Story of the Pipa* lies in the fact that Gao Ming did not avoid the three weaknesses displayed by Cai Bojie; his failure to serve his parents when they were alive, to bury his parents when they died, and to offer a sacrifice to his parents after their burial. Instead, Gao Ming makes the audience sympathize with Cai Bojie, despite his failings. In this way, Gao succeeded in establishing a new kind of aesthetic, which fused scholarly philosophy with the concerns of common people. In this way, *Story of the Pipa* changed the ethical values of the plays about ungrateful scholars common in *xiwen* during the Song and Yuan dynasties. However it also changed their structures. *Story of the Pipa* consists of forty-two scenes, breaking with the four act pattern of Yuan *zaju*, which was constrained by its musical system.

Gao Ming was able to begin the play in a more dramatic way. The parallel storylines heralded a new, dual plot structure for *chuanqi*

The Kunqu Opera *A Wooden Hairpin* performed by the Jiangsu Kunqu Troupe. Here, Aunt Qian receives betrothal gifts from Sun's and Wang's families in Yulian's bedroom. She speaks highly of Sun's wealth, but Yulian insists on choosing the wooden hairpin from Wang's family.

and its influence completely changed the cultural status of *xiwen*.
Zhu Yuanzhang, the first emperor of the Ming Dynasty (who reigned
from 1368–1398) thought highly of the play, and claimed "If four
books and five classics are daily necessities, as necessary as food and
clothing, then *Story of the Pipa* is like a delicacy that wealthy or noble
families cannot do without."

Due to the success of *Story of the Pipa*, Song *xiwen* scripts were
elevated and soon replaced Yuan *zaju*, becoming the most influential
operatic form in China during the Ming and Qing dynasties. With
Story of the Pipa, Chinese opera entered mainstream culture.

The status of *xiwen* was further consolidated by the emergence
of four plays, *A Wooden Hairpin (Jing Chai Ji)*, *White Rabbit (Bai Tu
Ji)*, *Praying to the Moon (Bai Yue Ji)*, and *Killing the Dog (Sha Gou Ji)*
which were the most important operas to follow *Story of the Pipa*.

A Wooden Hairpin tells the story of a young woman named Qian
Yulian who refuses to marry a rich suitor, Sun Ruquan, and instead
marries Wang Shipeng, a scholar whose betrothal gift to Qian is a
wooden hairpin. Once they are married, Wang goes to the capital
to take the imperial examination and successfully passes. Moqi's
daughter wants to marry Wang but he refuses and is banished.
Problems arise when Sun Ruquan changes a letter from Wang
to Qian Yulian, making it into request for a divorce. As a result,
Qian Yulian's stepmother forces Qian to remarry. Qian refuses and
jumps into the river, but is saved by Qian Zaihe, a newly appointed
local official. Believing that Wang is dead, Qian Zaihe adopts Qian
Yulian as his daughter, taking her to his official residence. Both
Qian Yulian and Wang believe the other to be dead, but still pine
for each other. Fortuitously the two meet by the river while offering
sacrifices for the other.

White Rabbit is also known as *Liu Zhiyuan*. It is based on a play
from the Tang Dynasty, *Zhu Gongdiao of Liu Zhiyuan*. It tells the
story of Liu Zhiyuan who leaves home to join the army while his
wife, Sanniang, is tortured at home by his brother and sister-in-
law. Sanniang gives birth to a son in a mill. Using her mouth to

The Shaoxing Opera *White Rabbit*, performed by Zhejiang Wenzhou Shaoxing Opera Troupe. In this scene Sanniang and her son are reunited after fifteen years of separation.

sever the umbilical cord, she names him Yaojilang, meaning "one whose umbilical chord was bitten off." She asks Dou Gong to send her son to Liu Zhiyuan. Fifteen years later, Liu Zhiyuan instructs his son to return to his mother. The son does not know where to find her mother, until he meets her drawing water from a well as he is hunting a white rabbit. Liu Zhiyuan eventually returns to the village with his men and is reunited with his wife.

Praying to the Moon is also known as *Story of the Quiet Bower* (*You Ge Ji*). It is adapted from Guan Hanqing's *The Pavilion of Praying to the Moon*. In Guan Hanqing's play the story takes place amidst the ravages and turmoil of war, where Jiang Shilong and Wang Ruilan meet while fleeing to safety and get married. The best parts of this work were incorporated into the southern *xiwen Praying to the Moon*. The characters' librettos are simple and vivid, maintaining the essence of the original work.

The Kunqu Opera *Killing the Dog*, performed by the Zhejiang Yongjia Conservatory of Kunqu Opera.

Killing the Dog also developed from an earlier Yuan *zaju*, *Killing the Dog to Persuade the Husband* (*Sha Gou Quan Fu*). Sun Hua, the son of a wealthy family, plots with two local thugs named Liu Longqing and Hu Zichuan, to drive his brother Sun Rong out of the family. Sun Hua's wife Yang Yuezhen tries to persuade him against the plan but fails, so she kills a dog, puts it in a bag, and places it outside the gate of their house. Sun Hua returns home late at night and is frightened. He asks Liu Longqing and Hu Zichuan for help but they avoid him. The only one willing to help is Sun Rong, whose brotherly affection is stronger than that of Sun Hua's so-called friends. A classic story from the Song and Yuan dynasties, the detailed portrayal of family affection as well as the portrayal of Liu Longqing and Hu Zichuan was especially vivid.

Along with *Story of the Pipa* these four southern *xiwen* marked the beginning of the *chuanqi*, a new era in the development of Chinese opera.

Kunqu Opera and the Exquisite *Peony Pavilion*

The word *chuanqi* came into usage during the Tang Dynasty, when it referred to short stories. However when *xiwen* emerged during the Song and Yuan dynasties, the word *chuanqi* was used to describe an operatic style of narration.

From the Song Dynasty's *The No.1 Scholar Zhang Xie* through to the early Yuan *Story of the Pipa*, operatic plays shared similarities with *zaju*. They consisted of complete narratives told through music alternated with dramatic monologues, and *qupai* (melodies) lyrically represented the central characters.

However, these operas differed from the four-act *zaju*, where the *qupai* used in each act was set by a given formula determined by the palace. The *qupai* selected for *chuanqi* were more flexible. From *The No.1 Scholar Zhang Xie* (which is not divided into different acts) to *Story of the Pipa* (which consisted of forty-two scenes), *xiwen* no longer followed the predetermined musical scores of *zaju*.

The new characteristics of *xiwen* (commonly known as *chuanqi* during the Ming Dynasty) broke conventions on the kind of tunes and number of acts operas had, prioritizing dramatic features above musical requirements.

Chuanqi's musical styles were thus harder to regulate than those of *zaju*. The creators of *chuanqi* were mainly scholars, who sought a means of expression which could be directly reflected in the music. Wei Liangfu, of Taicang, Jiangsu, created exquisite Kunshan tunes, which became the archetypal tune of *chuanqi* of the Ming Dynasty.

Song and Yuan *xiwen* had developed in the Zhejiang region in the south, the product of local folk customs and musical forms.

Similarly, *chuanqi* of the Ming Dynasty developed in the southern regions where a variety of tunes sprang up, including the

Haiyan tune near Hangzhou in Zhejiang and the Yiyang tune in Jiangxi. These tunes replaced northern *zaju*.

When Wei Liangfu created the Kunshan tune, he modified the original arias of the Yiyang and Haiyan tunes, combining the rhythms of southern *xiwen*, which favored the flute, and the styles of northern *zaju*, which favored plucked string instruments.

The opera *Washing Silken Gauze* (*Huan Sha Ji*) by Liang Chenyu, marked the beginning of Kunqu Opera, which employs the Kunshan tune throughout.

Liang Chenyu, an important sixteenth-century dramatist, was born in Kunshan, Jiangsu. *Washing Silken Gauze* was based on *Spring and Autumn of the States of Wu and Yue* (*Wu Yue Chun Qiu*). It consists of forty-five scenes that explore the competition between the states of Wu and Yue. The State of Wu defeats the State of Yue,

The Kunqu Opera *Washing Silken Gauze*, performed by Northern Kunqu Troupe.

The revival scene from the Kunqu Opera *Peony Pavilion*. Liu Mengmei opens Du Lininag's tomb and she is brought back to life. The two then get married.

and King Goujian of Yue adopts a strategy devised by Fan Li, a senior official, to concede defeat and offer great gifts to the King of Wu, which include sending Fan Li's beautiful fiancée Xi Shi.

Following his victory, the King of Wu neglects state affairs while King Goujian lives a poor and hard life. In the end, the State of Yue becomes strong and overcomes its humiliation.

The author abandoned the simplicity of Yuan *zaju* in favor of elegant, rhetorically complex lines. The opera integrated the exquisite *shuimo* tune ("water mill" tune), attracting the praise of a generation of scholars.

From this point onwards, *chuanqi*-style operas followed the norms of the Kunshan tune. *Chuanqi* performed with the Kunshan tune appealed to scholarly tastes and this elegant music gained a special cultural status. Other local tunes of the same period were, by comparison, considered vulgar.

From the beginning of the mid-Ming Dynasty, Kunqu Opera began to spread widely, becoming a symbol of Chinese culture.

In *Interrupted Dream*, the 1960 film version of *Peony Pavilion*, the role of Du Liniang is played by the famous Peking Opera actor Mei Lanfang (on the right). Lanfang's student Yan Huizhu plays the role of Chunxiang.

Chuanqi reached its artistic peak through the writings of Tang Xianzu (1550–1616). Tang Xianzu, a famous Ming Dynasty scholar, was well-known for his *Four Dreams at Linchuan*, four outstanding plays that displayed his great literary talent. The four plays were *Tale of the Wooden Hairpin* (*Jing Chai Ji*), *Peony Pavilion* (*Mu Dan Ting*), *Nanke Dream* (*Nan Ke Ji*) and *Handan Dream* (*Han Dan Ji*). They shared the common theme of dreaming. *Peony Pavilion*, also known as *Revival of Du Liniang* (*Huan Hun Ji*), is perhaps the most outstanding *chuanqi* of the Ming Dynasty.

Peony Pavilion consists of fifty-five scenes and focuses on the erotic desires of Du Liniang, the daughter of Du Bao, governor of Nan'an. Du Liniang dreams of a young scholar she meets in a Peony Pavilion. Deeply moved by this dream, she takes a stroll in the garden and suddenly falls ill. She paints self-portraits and writes a poem, instructing her maid to hide these under a stone by the plum tree at Taihu Lake.

Shortly after, Du Liniang dies and is buried by the plum tree in the garden. Three years later, a scholar named Liu Mengmei comes to town to participate in the imperial examination. He falls ill and seeks a cure in a small shrine, finding the painting of a beautiful girl—Du Liniang. That night, he dreams of her and in his dream Liniang asks him to revive her. Opening her coffin, Liu Mengmei revives Du Liniang. The two lovers decide to get married and go to the capital—Lin'an (present-day Hangzhou).

Liu Mengmei visits Liniang's father Du Bao, and tells him that he has revived his daughter. However Du Bao accuses Liu Mengmei of being a grave robber, captures him and sends him to Lin'an. Unexpectedly, Liu Mengmei wins first place in the imperial examination but Du Bao refuses to accept his daughter's marriage, considering her to be a devil. However, the emperor himself believes Du Linaing and allows the marriage.

The distinctiveness of *Peony Pavilion* lies in its representation of Du Liniang's life and death. A young girl dreams of a lover, a figment of her imagination, but is then revived by the man of her

The Kunqu Opera *Peony Pavilion*, performed by the Suzhou Kunqu Troupe.

dreams years later. Du Liniang dies for her dream lover, and is
revived by a real, loyal lover.

This curious story explores the limits of life and death. Tang
Xianzu's lyrics sparkle with life, for example in his description of
Du Liniang's erotic desires and hidden bitterness:

> *Already, bright purple and passion pink bloom in profusion,
> yet next to a crumbling well and faded walls, such splendor is
> abandoned. But in this glorious season, where are the sounds of joy
> in this garden? Mornings take wing, evenings unfold; beyond green
> arbor, rosy clouds soar. In windy strands of rain, gilded pleasure
> boats nod in misty waves. Maidens shielded by screens, are blinded to
> such glorious scenes!*
>
> *All over the verdant hill, the azaleas are in full bloom. Beyond
> trellis vines, silky mist softly lingers. The peony is beuatiful, but
> blooms late when spring is gone.*

Peony Pavilion marks the peak of artistic achievement in *chuanqi* of the Ming and Qing dynasties. Despite displaying less precision in terms of Tang Xianzu's mastery of the rhythms of Kunqu Opera, a fact which drew the criticism and taunts of dramatists with a more familiar command of these rhythms, *Peony Pavilion* is an extraordinary tale which quickly became one of the most popular Kunqu Operas.

Other examples of Kunqu Operas which were widespread at this time include *The Schoolroom* (*Gui Shu*), *Interrupted Dream* (*Jing Meng*), *Pursuing the Dream* (*Xun Meng*), *The Portrait* (*Xie Zhen*), *Soul Departs* (*Li Hun*), *Infernal Judgment* (*Ming Pan*), *Finding the Portrait* (*Shi Hua*), *Union in the Shades* (*You Gou*), *The Pledge* (Ming Shi), and *Return to Life* (Huan Hun).

Palace of Eternity and *Peach Blossom Fan*

A very popular Kunqu Opera of the mid-Ming Dynasty was *Palace of Eternity* (*Chang Sheng Dian*) by Hong Sheng (1645-1704), who was born in Qiantang, Zhejiang. Despite his exceptional literary talent, Sheng had a hard life, and he drifted to the capital to make a living selling scripts. Hong Sheng's masterpiece *Palace of Eternity* took more than ten years of complete. The final version, which emerged from two earlier drafts (the first entitled *Chenxiang Pavilion*, and the second *Performing the Rainbow skirt and Feathered Cap Dance*), consisted of fifty different scenes which took two days to perform.

Palace of Eternity is a love story about Li Longji, Emperor Minghuang of the Tang Dynasty and his concubine Yang Yuhuan, and the troubled times in which they lived. It portrays the national outcry which resulted from Li Longji's excessive love for Yang Yuhuan. The first half of the opera focuses on portraying their love and the licentious behavior of Yuhan's brother, Yang Guozhong.

In the "Tribute of Litchi" scene, Li Longji orders the use of a swift horse to pay tribute from Litchi to Yang Yuhuan day and night from the south. The scene is a direct reflection of national complaints.

The Kunqu Opera *Palace of Eternity*, performed by the Suzhou Kunqu Troupe.

In taking Yang Yuhuan as his concubine, Li Longji breaks with palace decrees and his love leads him to abandon state affairs, provoking the rebellion of An Lushan. Li Longji makes a hasty escape from Chang'an, but his army mutinies and his officers ask the emperor to kill the treacherous court official Yang Guozhong and his sister Yang Yuhuan. Li Longji is left with no choice but to order Yang Yuhuan to kill herself. Li Longji spends the rest of his life mourning the loss of his love, and passes the throne to the prince.

The playwright and composer Hong Sheng places most of the opera's emphasis on the twists and turns of the love between Li Longji and Yang Yuhuan. The most important scene of the opera is perhaps the moment when the lovers first meet at the Palace of Eternity during the Double Seventh Festival, and secretly vow to stay together.

Yang Yuhuan and Li Longji were in two different worlds. "Though heaven and earth are long, they will cease at last, while regret finds no ending." This is an eternal tragedy.

Palace of Eternity, performed by the Zhejiang Hangzhou Kunqu Troupe on December 24, 2004, the 360th anniversary of the birth of Hong Sheng.

Palace of Eternity is a great work. Through portraying the conflict between politics and love, the play places its characters, particularly the Emperor Minghuang, in an intense confrontation with the fact that conciliation is impossible. Li Longji has no way of protecting his much-loved concubine and instead must witness her death.

The palace, with its numerous concubines, is not an environment conducive to sincere love, and so the love that flourishes between Li Longji and Yang Yuhuan is all the more admirable.

Hong Sheng's outstanding literary talent is evident in *Palace of Eternity*'s precise lyrics, which closely follow the melodic lines of the music.

When the script of *Palace of Eternity* appeared, it was quickly staged and gained popularity because "whoever loves literature likes its lyrics, and whoever knows music likes its rhythms." It became the favorite play of scholars and gentlemen, and actors competed to be able to perform in it.

However, Hong Sheng and some of his company were punished after the play came out because *Palace of Eternity* was illegally performed before the end of the mourning period for Empress Tong, the mother of Emperor Kangxi (who reigned from 1662–1722). Several of the company were expelled, including Sheng, who was exiled to his hometown. He died by drowning whilst drunk, as he was on his way to visit some friends.

Another great opera was *Peach Blossom Fan* (*Tao Hua Shan*), which, along with the *Palace of Eternity*, was one of the most

significant operas of the early Qing Dynasty. It was written by
Kong Shangren (1648–1718), who was born in Qufu, Shandong and
was a descendent of Confucius (551–479 BC).

Completed in the thirty-eighth year (1699) of the reign of
Kangxi, the play consists of forty scenes and four auxiliary scenes.

The late Ming Dynasty was a time of social unrest, fuelled by the
Li Zicheng Uprising, which was caused by a widespread famine.
When the army of the Qing Dynasty entered the Shanhaiguan Pass,
the Ming Dynasty collapsed. Through these events a generation
of scholars were forced to question their core social values. The
troubled times brought an end to their previously carefree lives in
which they had freely enjoyed song and dance, poems and wine.
The change of dynasty forced a change in their way of life. Scholars
in the south came into conflict with the new Qing court. Many
well-known scholars were reluctant to serve as officials and one
after another rose against the Qing Dynasty in various regions.

Having lived through the nation's troubles, Kong Shangren
described the changing times in his opera, which portrayed the
relationship between Hou Fangyu and other members of the
Donglin Party, including the cunning official Ruan Dacheng.

The opera's themes reverberated with scholars and the people
suffering from the collapse of the regime because, in Kong
Shangren's words, it "Draws an analogy between a romantic story
of parting and reunion and the rise and fall of an empire."

The opera begins with the narrator who describes his thoughts
on the actions of various characters, "Ah! How it made me weep,
laugh, rage, even curse!" The narrator's feelings reflect those of the
audience, as well as those of the author himself.

Peach Blossom Fan drew on the features of other *chuanqi* from
the Ming and Qing dynasties through the male and female
lead roles, which excelled in expressing the love between men
and women. The story of the love between Hou Fangyu and
Li Xiangjun, the hero and heroine, reflects the tremendous
transformations brought about by the change in the dynasties;
their gentle love songs contrast with the tumult of the dynastic

The Kunqu Opera *Peach Blossom Fan*, performed by Jiangsu Kunqu Troupe.

change, whilst in the merrier songs and dances of scholars and singing girls, the play expresses the painful meaning of the story against the backdrop of troubled times.

Peach Blossom Fan follows the love between the scholar Hou Fangyu and singer Li Xiangjun, by the Qinhuai River. Although Li Xiangjun is a singer, her emotions and actions are shown to be more noble than those of the scholars. She refuses to accept the gifts of Ruan Dacheng, a cunning and corrupt scholar, and she encourages Hou Fangyu to join the army in order to serve the nation. After Hou Fangyu leaves, Ruan Dacheng tries to force Li Xiangjun to marry another man. She refuses, falls to the ground and hits her head in an attempt to commit suicide. Her blood splatters on a poem Hou Fangyu had given her when they first met. Hou Fangyu's friend Yang Longyou then uses the blood

to paint a peach blossom on a fan. The poem and fan become a
symbol of Li Xiangjun's determination and integrity.

The Southern Ming regime finally falls and Li Xiangjun becomes
a nun. Hou Fangyu returns to look for her but, failing to find her,
becomes a monk. Although they meet again, their love is no longer.

The opera portrays the tensions between family ties, love, and
politics.

Enlightened master Zhao Yaoxing reprimands Hou for his love
for Li: "When there are such tremendous changes, you still indulge
in love? It is really ridiculous!" and "Where now is the nation? The
home? The prince? The father? But for this infatuation, can you not
get rid of it?"

The opera ends with the renouncing of family ties, but
withdrawing from society and living in obscurity is not what the
author wanted to advocate. What the end of the opera represents

The Kunqu Opera *Peach Blossom Fan*.

is the sense of powerlessness portrayed throughout. Knowing that the Ming Dynasty was doomed to fall, scholars were eager to serve the nation, but in reality they are helpless to do anything about it. The opera's message, therefore, is not a religious one but a philosophical comment on the insignificance of scholars at a time when an empire was coming to an end.

It is with a hint of irony that *Peach Blossom Fan* follows the romances of various scholars. Simple and honest, and unwilling to become involved with corrupt officials, the scholars appear respectable, but they inevitably end up working for the officials. In stark contrast, after Hou Fangyu leaves, Li Xiangjun insists on saving herself for him. Having worked as a prostitute by the Qinhuai River, her fidelity to Hou is a more staunch show of loyalty and moral integrity than that shown by the scholars at a time when the nation was in great peril. Although in comparison with the fall of the emperor her fate is insignificant, the seemingly disconnected plots represent the author's despair at the fall of the state through the love and loss of the hero and heroine.

Palace of Eternity and *Peach Blossom Fan* were both works based on real historical events and their success inspired other writers who copied the seriousness and political material of these two operas. Purely fictional operas such as Peony Pavilion began to fall out of favor.

Li Yu and Kunqu Opera Stage Performances

Kunqu Opera developed from humble origins into a grand theatrical form based the performance system of *xiwen*, refining the roles used in Song and Yuan *xiwen* and Yuan *zaju*.

Performers of Kunqu Opera came from all walks of life and belonged to professional troupes or family-based troupes, set up by scholars and officials. In these troupes, actors, writers and musicians converged, enabling the development of Kunqu Opera's celebrated style. In just a few hundred years, Kunqu Opera had incorporated traditional music, dance and literature and thus it encompasses all of the main Chinese cultural forms.

In the Han, Tang, and Song dynasties as well as the Ming and Qing dynasties, there were three kinds of performance venues for Chinese opera. The first type were halls in the palaces and houses of rich merchants and the aristocracy; the second kind were tiled roof houses or open spaces next to the road; the third type were stages at village temples in rural areas.

The performances in the palace and halls were identical in nature. Performers in these could be divided into two categories: Palace performers, such as those from educational institutions set up in the Han, Tang and Song dynasties and those from family troupes run by scholars and aristocrats during the Ming and Qing dynasties. These performances targeted specific audiences.

Performers had no commercial considerations and what was performed was decided by the hosts. Performances put on in private residences, however, required higher quality performers.

During the Ming and Qing dynasties public performances developed rapidly. These performances were staged in various venues, including the palace halls of aristocrats and nobles, where they formed part of the entertainment at feasts. They started appearing in commercial business premises and eventually became the mainstay of urban opera performances.

It was on this wave of development that Suzhou playwrights such as Li Yu (1591–1671) flourished. These writers were mostly middle-class scholars who had a good command of the Suzhou dialect and could write operas that catered for the mass market as Kunqu Opera expanded in Suzhou, the area south of the Yangtze River.

The settings and language their scripts employed distinguished them from scripts written by more well-known scholars, so that a new style of *chuanqi* was created.

Li Yu lived during the late Ming and early Qing dynasties. He was born into a humble family in Wuxian, Jiangsu. Li Yu did not attend the imperial examinations. He had no intention of seeking official rank and devoted his life to researching and writing opera.

His plays can be found in up to forty-two different opera anthologies. The most well known are his four masterpieces: *Snow White Cup* (*Yi Peng Xue*), *Between Man and Beast* (*Ren Shou Guan*), *Together Forever* (*Yong Tuan Yuan*), and *Winning the Beauty Queen* (*Zhan Hua Kui*).

Snow White Cup consists of thirty scenes. The name of the play is taken from a legendary jade cup of the Ming Dynasty, which would keep wine cool in summer and warm wine in winter. It was said that when a good wine was poured, snowflakes would fly from the cup and so it was named "Snow White Cup."

The play tells the story of the cup, which is handed down through the family of Mo Huaigu, a high official of the Court of Imperial Sacrifices. During the Jia Jing Period of the Ming Dynasty, Minister Yan Song and his son were overbearing and unscrupulously plundered rare jade wares from around the world.

In the story, Yan and Mo are old family friends. Mo Huaigu recommends Tang Qin, his family's antiques dealer, to Yan Song's son Yan Shifan. The evil Tang Qin encourages Yan Shifan to steal the jade cup from Mo Huaigu. Mo Huaigu tries to pass off a fake but Tang Qin sees through the ploy and Yan Shifan searches Mo's residence.

Mo Huaigu loses office and flees but Yan's family eventually arrest him. Jizhou General Qi Jiguang is ordered to behead Mo Huaigu but Mo Cheng, his loyal servant, agrees to take his master's place and Mo Huaigu escapes.

The head of Mo Cheng is delivered to the capital and Tang Qin realizes that he has been tricked. Court guard Lu Bing is ordered to investigate. However, Lu Bing discovers that Tang Qin intends to kidnap Mo Huaigu's wife, Xueyan. Following a hint from Xueyan, Lu Bing pretends to suspect that Xueyan is to be given to Tang Qin as a concubine. Tang Qin drops his investigation and Xueyan pretends to accept this but uses the opportunity to kill Tang Qin and commits suicide after taking revenge for Mo's family.

Xueyan then raises Mo Cheng's son Wenlu and Mo Huaigu returns to Jinzhou. He meets his wife as she and Wenlu are offering a sacrifice for him outside the west gate. The couple formally adopt Wenlu and the family is reunited.

Snow White Cup dramatically contrasts the behavior of Tang Qing, who betrays his friend for his own gain, and the humble actions of the servant Mo Cheng and the concubine Xueyan. Many scenes, including "Trial of Head" and "Killing Tang Qin" are still performed on stage today and remain popular.

Li Yu's operas *Snow White Cup, Together Forever, Between Man and Beast* and *Winning the Beauty Queen* are all about common people. Their sympathetic portrayal was so popular that Li Yu was one of the first writers able to make a living by writing operas.

The Peking Opera *Snow White Cup*. Ma Changli plays the role of Mo Huaigu.

Li Yu's later operas focused more on the political and social struggles of the late Ming and early Qing dynasties. Among these plays were *Roster of the Loyal and Pure* (*Qing Zhong Pu*) and *The Tragic Killing of the Loyalists* (*Qian Zhong Lu*), which both displayed a high level of dramatic tension.

The Tragic Killing of the Loyalists is about Zhu Di, prince of Yan, who launches the Battle of Jingnan in the early Ming Dynasty. His army marches southward and sets the imperial capital of Nanjing on fire. Encouraged by his courtiers, the Emperor Jianwen disguises himself as a monk and flees. As he hurriedly leaves the capital, his anxiety and loneliness resulting from the unexpected turn of events, are expressed in an aria:

> *Put together the wonderful mountains and rivers, all the four elements are void. Having experienced a long journey, thick forests, high mountains, and the rolling waves of the Yangtze River... The country looks safe and sound, but who knows I came to Xiangyang alone with only a wooden ladle and a straw hat.*

The Kunqu Opera *The Killing of the Loyalists*. Yu Zhenfei plays the role of Emperor Jianwen.

Kunqu Operas of the Ming Dynasty, with lyrics and themes focused on love, represented the pursuit of sultriness among scholars during the Ming Dynasty. They failed to express their more open minds. The emergence of Li Yu led to changes in *chuanqi* during the Ming Dynasty and infused more diverse masculine styles.

Another timeless opera of the early Qing Dynasty is *Story of Xiong Youlan and Xiong Youhui* (*Shuang Xiong Meng*) by Zhu Suchen.

Story of Xiong Youlan and Xiong Youhui, later known as *Fifteen Strings of Coins* (*Shi Wu Guan*), skillfully employs the double plot structure of the *chuanqi* classics of the Ming and Qing dynasties. The story focuses on how the brothers were involved in a murder linked to fifteen strings of bronze coins. A cunning official judges the case and mistakenly involves two innocent women. When the four suspects seem to be unavoidably heading towards punishment, the righteous official Kuang Zhong finds flaws in the case and carefully investigates. He eventually arrests the murderer and proves the four people to be innocent.

The misfortunes of the four characters link them and the connections between life and death underscore the uncertainties of life.

The Kunqu Opera *Fifteen Strings of Cash*.

The operas of Li Yu (1611–1680) were also notable. Among them are *Cherishing a Fragrant Companion (Lian Xiang Ban)*, *A Wrong Kite (Feng Zheng Wu)*, *Pavilion in the Mirage (Shen Zhong Lou)*, and *Flatfish (Bi Mu Yu)*. Li Yu was one of the most important opera theorists in Chinese history. He researched and wrote about Kunqu Opera, taught family troupes to perform his plays, and carefully preserved his scripts. His operas are mostly romantic stories, but rather than dwelling on profound thoughts or feelings, his tales were lively and entertaining, exploiting all the elements of Kunqu Opera. In this he bridged the gap between scholarly elegance and folk styles.

Promoted by scholars, the influence of Kunqu Opera has been extensive. Actors are still subject to social discrimination, but the art of opera, on the whole, is now considered to be an elegant part of culture. The cultural significance of Kunqu Opera needs to be set in a broader social context beyond the realm of opera to be fully understood and explained.

Flowers in Bloom: Chinese Opera Diversifies

The Spread of Yiyang and Clapper Opera

Whilst Kunqu Opera had won favor among middle and upper-class nobles and trademen, in rural areas with relatively low levels of economic development, the ornate diction and courtly elegance of Kunqu did not appeal to the more rustic performers of folk opera.

From the Yuan Dynasty to the Ming Dynasty, folk operas had developed significantly and their colorful forms flourished and invigorated an already diversified Chinese opera.

Tunes such as Haiyan, Yuyao and Yiyang emerged from Jiangsu and Zhejiang in the south of China, local tunes which gradually replacing northern *zaju*. The more sophisticated and elegant Kunshan tune which later emerged, drew on the brilliance of these earlier forms without reproducing them completely. The popular southern *Yiyang* tune fused with the Kunqu Opera as it spread to other regions, so that the two forms evolved in parallel.

An ancient opera stage built in 1749 in Wuzheng, Zhejiang. Such stages can be found throughout China.

In the eyes of the literati, the Yiyang tune was clearly different from the Kunshan tune. Due to the strict regulation of the rhythms of southern and northern operas instigated by Wei Liangfu, it was easy to develop rhythms and narratives for the Kunshan tune and these were used to regulate and teach performers.

The spread of *chuanqi* scripts and Kunqu Opera pleased scholars who noted the increasingly complex aesthetic of the Kunshan tune. The Yiyang tune should have achieved the same position as Kunshan tune, but with a lack of masters like Wei Liangfu, able to develop and set out its rhythmical rules, the Yiyang tune changed constantly as it spread.

Thus, a wide variety of high-pitched tunes spread from south to north, the product of the convergence between the Yiyang tune and local dialects and musical styles, fusions which were enabled by Yiyang's unregulated rhythms.

Unlike the slow and elegant Kunshan tune that could be sung softly and quietly, the Yiyang tune had a rougher quality. Yiyang tunes were sung without orchestral instruments or other vocal accompaniment. It relied largely on the strength of single voice to express dramatic emotions at a time when opera performances had yet to synchronize fully vocal and instrumental harmonies.

The stories enacted through the Yiyang tune concerned familial loyalty and faithfulness, integrity and righteousness, and were coupled with impassioned, exciting music. Its uninhibited, bawdy style appealed to the lower classes and reflected the capabilities of the actors and musicians who performed it. In rural areas, operas were often staged on open-air temple stages with simple facilities.

The high-pitched tune
The high-pitched tune is one of four classic tunes in traditional Chinese opera. The other three are the Kunshan tune, the Clapper tune and the Pihuang tune. The High-pitched tune is characterized by simple performances of high-pitched singing. Singers are accompanied by a gold drum. From the mid-Ming Dynasty onwards, it began to spread from Jiangxi to the rest of the country. Different styles of high-pitched tune emerged in different parts of the country, including Hubei, Hunan and Sichuan, Yunnan, as well as Beijing and other provinces.

The Sichuan Opera *Story of Burning Incense.*

From the Song and Yuan dynasties onwards, opera performances had been based on roughly fixed musical forms, whether *xiwen*, *zaju* or Kunqu Opera. However, the Yiyang tune spread among ordinary people and did not follow these strict rules, allowing folk artists the freedom to create new forms.

During the mid-Ming Dynasty, the Yiyang tune incrementally deviated from its originally fixed scripts, breaking with convention and changing the nature of opera through the many varieties of high-pitched tunes which evolved from it.

Operas with their own regional styles sprang up in the south and north and became the mainstay of local performances. The Yiyang tune had a significant influence on dozens of these operas, marking it out as one of the most influential forms in the development of Chinese folk opera.

The sheer quantity and distribution of operas with high-pitched tunes demonstrates the scope of Yiyang's spread.

The emergence of Shaanxi Opera in the northwestern part of China was another important musical development.

Shaanxi Opera, which emerged in the central Shaanxi plain, based its central aria on the Quanshan aria already popular in the region. Whereas Kunqu Opera's high-pitched tunes were based on

The Shaanxi Opera *Yang Qiniang*.

the strictly regulated long and short lines of *qupai*, Shaanxi Opera had two kinds of melodic lines; lines with seven Chinese characters and lines with ten. A musical unit consisted of two lines of the same number of characters, a couplet, which was a common form in various local operas.

For example in *The Lotus in the Earthen Bowl* (*Bo Zhong Lian*), a recently discovered opera which was performed in the south during the Wanli Period (1573–1620) of the Ming Dynasty, there is a section which uses couplets of seven or ten-character lines.

Shaanxi Opera introduced a brand new style of musical singing to Chinese opera known as the *banqiang* style. Hanju Opera, Peking Opera, Cantonese Opera, Shaoxing Opera, Pingju Opera and Huangmei Opera are all based on the *banqiang* style. With a simple structure and distinct rhythms, *banqiang* style was easy to master and suitable for most folk opera performances. Its simplicity enabled many changes to be made to its form.

Although Shaanxi Opera takes the two-six-beat style from the *quanshan* aria as the basis for singing, it retained quite a few of its

Quanshan **aria**
Quanshan aria was the most common folk form in the central Shaanxi plain. It was used in Taoism to convey religious teachings at temple fairs and folk events during the Ming and Qing dynasties. Taoist quanshan arias are still performed today and remain concerned with moral enlightenment. Tales like *Twenty-four Stories* about faithfulness to family have lyrics that follow the seven and ten-character line structure.

tunes. However, these tunes are generally not suitable for singing and many are used in the overture, during the interval or as musical accompaniment during the performance.

A clapper-based instrumental accompaniment system emerged in Shaanxi Opera. By the mid-Qing Dynasty, percussion music had gradually evolved so that drumbeats were supplemented by metal instruments such as cymbals and gongs, leading to gong and drum ensembles. Before a Shaanxi Opera performance, drums and gongs were used as the prelude, particularly in open-air venues, to create an atmosphere and attract large audiences before a performance.

During performances, different gong and drum ensembles were used at various times to create special effects and add dramatic tension. Shaanxi Opera is known as clapper opera because clappers at different pitches would lead the rest of the orchestra, along with the conductor.

An independent and well-developed style, Shaanxi Opera spread around the country. Its spread was assisted by the Li Zicheng Uprising of 1629 which resulted in the fall of Beijing in 1644 and the subsequent overthrow the Ming Dynasty.

Shaanxi farmers who became soldiers were the mainstay of Li Zicheng's troops, and they were said to have taken Shaanxi Opera as their military motif, causing many Shaanxi Opera performers to join them. Wherever they went, they would celebrate big victories with a Shaanxi Opera performance at the local temple of Guan Yu. When defeated, the Shaanxi Opera performers, along with the troops, would scatter, enabling the rapid spread of Shaanxi Opera.

As the style spread, it combined with local musical forms to create new styles of clapper opera.

Shaanxi Opera was completely different from Kunqu Opera in terms of its musical style, which was more accessible to ordinary people, although in both forms love was the most popular theme.

In 1779, the famous Shaanxi Opera performer Wei Changsheng (1744–1802) came to Beijing to perform *Wallowing on the Floor* (Gun Lou). In the opera she played a girl who, opposed to the behavior of the court, becomes a bandit. One night, she sleeps in the same room as Wang Ziying, a defeated general. The general and the girl come to love each other and decide to marry. They are married immediately in a traditional Chinese marriage ceremony.

Wei Changsheng used graceful body language and charming expressions to portray the strength of both the love and the hate which the leading female character feels, as well as a kind of emotional shyness. Wei's bold yet delicate performance was deeply moving. The actress took Shaanxi Opera performances into a new realm. As this style became increasingly popular among Beijing audiences, actresses in various other regions began to copy her style.

A Shaanxi Opera performance in a village.

Competition between Huabu and Yabu

In Yangzhou, an important commercial port near Suzhou during the Qing Dynasty, opera performances were stimulated by the presence of Huizhou merchants and by a tour by Emperor Qianlong (1736–1795). Various regional tunes challenged the mainstream cultural performances of Kunqu Opera resulting in a local competition between Huabu and Yabu.

Yabu encompassed performances of Kunqu Opera, while Huabu included Shaanxi Operas, the Yiyang tune, Clapper Opera, the Luoluo tune and the Erhuang melody.

In Huabu (also known as Luantan), the most important and influential style was Peking Opera.

The rise of Peking Opera was linked to the Yangzhou Salt Commission, who organised opera performances. In the fifty-fifth year (1790) of Emperor Qianlong's reign, the imperial government gathered local theatrical troupes to perform in Beijing for the emperor's birthday. The Huizhou opera troupes from Yangzhou

Peking Opera Anhui Opera Troupes Come to Beijing, showing the grand event of four major Anhui Opera troupes' Beijing tour during the Qing Dynasty.

were the most popular. The top four Huizhou troupes which performed in Beijing staged operas with diverse tune patterns, which included Kunqu Opera, Clapper Opera, and the Erhuang melody. Their colorful performances gradually won the favor of audiences in Beijing and the imperial capital's opera performance scene become increasingly active.

A three-storey theatre in the Forbidden City in Beijing.

At the same time, Hanju Opera (popular along the Yangtze River and Hanshui River) also emerged. Hanju and Huizhou opera troupes complemented and mixed with each other and the result was Peking Opera, which encapsulated the essence of Beijing's cultural scene.

The growth and development of Peking Opera was closely related to performances at the imperial court. The Qing Dynasty established special schools and employed folk artists to teach eunuchs how to perform Kunqu Opera and Yiyang Tune Opera for emperors. After

The theatre in the palace of Prince Gong of the Qing Dynasty, built in 1777.

Portraits of Peking Opera characters played by famous actors of late Qing Dynasty. They were painted by Shen Rongpu, a well-known portraitist active in the late Qing period.

Teahouses
The teahouse was a typical venue for opera performances in Beijing during the late Qing Dynasty. Teahouses consisted of stages surrounded by tables. Tea and snacks were available, although the major function of teahouses was the performance of opera. Although entry charges were typically called tea payments, the performances were the primary attraction. The price of tea payments varied from seat to seat, depending on proximity to, and visibility of, the stage.

the mid-Qing Dynasty, emperors fond of operas invited singers to perform at the imperial palace. From the reign of Emperor Guangxu onwards, large numbers of troupes were invited to perform in the palace and famous performers took to the palace stage on various occasions, including birthday celebrations or grand ceremonies.

The Empress Dowager Cixi and Ci'an, Emperor Guangxu (reigned 1875–1908), gave outstanding Peking Opera performers rich rewards after performances. The folk artists originally employed to teach eunuchs, gradually took on the role of managing and organizing these performances.

The growth of opera as a common pastime among ordinary people had an even greater impact on the development of Peking Opera. The Qing Dynasty saw the rapid emergence of Bejing tea houses which staged Peking Operas. As the demand for performances grew, so did the number of troupes. These troupes were often led by well-known actors such as Peking

Opera male leads Cheng Changgeng (1811–1880), Yu Sansheng (1802–1866), and Zhang Erkui (1814–1860).

Peking Opera drew on a rich array of Chinese operas. Operas evolved from folk story-telling with the accompaniment of stringed instruments of the Tang and Song dynasties. *Romance of Three Kingdoms (San Guo Yan Yi)*, *Outlaws of the Marsh (Shui Hu Zhuan)*, *Investiture of the Gods (Feng Shen Bang)* and *Legend of the Flying Dragon (Fei Long Zhuan)* were all adapted into a large number of opera performances. The historical aspects of popular folk stories offered numerous elements that could be incorporated into stories that could be staged, and thus constituted the core theme of Chinese operas. Significantly different from Kunqu Opera's tendency to privilege stories about scholars and love, Peking Opera covered themes including national identity, judicial trials, good and evil and heroic legends, the latter proving very popular.

Whilst Peking Opera inherited many stories from Kunqu Opera, it was more influenced by Clapper Opera and other styles that had more resonance with common people.

The unique performance system of Peking Opera involved the performance of highlights from different operas.

Performances of *xiwen* or *zaju* lasted between three and six hours, the time it took to perform their complete narratives. In contrast, Peking Opera consisted of between five and ten operatic highlights, with the number depending on whether it was performed within the palace or outside, in the afternoon or in the evening.

The rapid development of Peking Opera was also attributable to renowned performing artists including Cheng Changgeng and Tan Xinpei (1847–1917).

Through performing in numerous classic Peking Operas, Tan Xinpei gained a reputation for his unique tone, which brilliantly conveyed the desolation felt by the tragic heroes he played. His most famous opera, *The Battle of Dingjunshan* (*Ding Jun Shan*), as well as other plays such as *Qin Qiong Sells His Horse* (*Qin Qiong Mai Ma*), *The Story of the Black Pot* (*Wu Pen Ji*), *A Child Left in the Mulberry Garden* (*Sang Yuan Ji Zi*), and *The Fourth Son of the Yang Family Visits His Mother* (*Si Lang Tan Mu*) created an enthusiasm amongst his audiences for operas which portrayed the

Tan Xinpei plays the role of Yang Yanhui in *The Fourth Son of the Yang Family Visits His Mother.*

The actor Tan Xinpei.

psychological state and plight of unsung heroes. Tan possessed a rare vocal capacity for compassionately portraying tragic figures and the hardships they faced.

In *Qin Qiong Sells His Horse* the hero Qin Qiong is forced to sell his favorite war horse. Time and again he expresses what the horse means to him but shakes his head and says "Just take it home with you, but I am not sure where it will settle down." Tan's voice expertly expressed Qin Qiong's frustration and it was his way of performing classic arias that lent this era its unique aesthetics. Tan Xinpei's performance style encapsulated traditional aesthetics: Complaining without anger and sadness without hurt, overflowing with a unique sense of decadence and the vicissitudes of life. A millennium-old empire's last gasp was perhaps shown more vividly in Tan Xinpei's voice than anywhere else.

Peking Opera was the product of the rivalry between Huabu and Yabu and was significant and popular enough to displace the culturally dominant position of Kunqu Opera. In other regions of China, such as Hubei, Sichuan, Jiangsu and Zhejiang, as well as neighboring Fujian along the Yangtze River basin and Shanxi, Henan and Shandong in North China, the spread of high-pitched tunes and Luantan generated a large number of operas with local tunes. The most important were Shanxi Opera, Henan Opera, Hebei Clapper Opera, Shandong Laizhou Clapper Opera, Cantonese Opera, Fujian Opera, Jiangxi Opera and Sichuan Opera. The emergence of these new operas signaled a new era of growth for Chinese theatre.

From Playlets to Full-Scale Operas

During the Han and Tang dynasties, early opera performances fell into two categories: *Ta-yao-niang* and Canjun opera. Folk songs and dances from various regions in the south and north emerged from the *Ta-yao-niang* style of opera. They were known (depending on the region) as Flower-Drum Opera, Flower-Lantern Opera, Tea-Picking Opera and *Yangge* Opera. These operas were performed at celebrations and religious festivals, and although they originated in folklore, as they evolved they became artistic entertainments in their own right. The folk songs and dances told short stories through distinctive local tunes sung by male and female performers.

Around 1900, performers of Huangxiao Flower-Drum Opera (popular in Hubei's Huangban and Xiaogan regions) began to enter Wuhan, a large city situated in the middle section of the Yangtze River, and put on complete plays in some of the tea houses in the city. From its origins in Wuhan, Huangxiao flower-drum opera grew over the next ten years into a new and popular opera style—Chuju Opera.

Huangxiao Flower-Drum Opera is a playlet (or short play) that included various local song and dance performances. It consisted of a simple plot with a male role and a female role—often called a two-role playlet. Such playlets focused on folk love stories, for example the *Longing for Twelve Months* (*Shi Er Xiang*), which tells the tale of a woman, Zhang Erjie, and her longing for Yu Laosi.

A Peking Opera performance in a tea house of the Qing Dynasty.

During the performance Yu Laosi comes onto the stage and Zhang and Yu sing in turn, from the first lunar month to the twelfth. During the performance, a bamboo curtain is used to separate them, representing their different locations in the play. They long for each other and complain about each other, each demonstrating both deep love and humor.

Small plays such as these gradually developed a more dramatic orientation, as can be seen in another two-role playlet *Aunt Wang asks after Zhang Erjie (Wang Da Niang Wen Bing)*, also known as *Outside the Window (Sha Chuang Wai)*. In this play Zhang is ill and Wang comes to look after her. Wang asks about the cause of her illness and Zhang answers through various arias. Eventually, Zhang reveals the source of her illness, which is her longing for a scholar.

The playlet developed into a flower-drum opera— *Wu Sanbao's Spring Tour (Wu San Bao You Chun)* in which the heroine, Zhao Saihua, encounters Wu Sanbao during a spring holiday. Wu deliberately drops his white fan and Zhao picks it up, returns home and becomes ill through her longing for Wu. Aunt Wang witnesses these events and goes to Zhao's to look after her, promising to find away for the couple to be together. Meanwhile, Wu is also sick, and Aunt Wang goes to look after him, knowing of Wu and Zhao's mutual love. Aunt Wang asks them both to come to her home to help them fulfill their wish to be together.

Because it evolved from folk songs and dances, Huangxiao flower-drum opera maintained the style of antiphonal singing between the male and female lead, long after it spread to the cities. Its lyrics and storylines, which combined bold expressions of passion with simple music, were distinctly those of

Two-Role playlet and Three-Role playlet
Alongside Song and Yuan *xiwen* and Yuan *zaju*, which had many character roles, smaller folk songs and dances were also performaned. These performances focused on two-role antiphonal singing by a young male and a young female, or by a clown and a young female and were known as two-role playlets. At times, there was a third part, which changed the atmosphere, creating a more dramatic space between the two main roles, which became known as the three-role playlet, which was performed by a young male, a young female and a clown. Both two-role and three-role playlets share some common features. Their lyrics roughly correspond to couplets. Their basic rhythms are generally simple and easy to remember and sing. Complicated techniques are not required. These playlets spread quickly and many new operas evolved from them.

The flower-drum opera *Selling Groceries* is a typical two-role playlet.

folk opera. It quickly won over most audiences and ultimately enriched the development of Chinese operas.

In the early twentieth century, folk storytelling and singing in the areas around Shanghai also began to evolve into operatic performances, producing many new works. Tanhuang, a form of opera from the south of the Yangtze River, was story-telling accompanied by drums. It emerged from the opera scripts of the Song Dynasty and was first performed in tea houses. It often focused on sexual scandals and so it was often prohibited by feudal officials and criticized by scholars. In the early twentieth century, some Tanhuang artists staged plays that ranged from naturalistic two-role playlets to stylized dramatic stage performances. In this way Tanhuang, as it was performed around Changzhou and Wuxi, evolved into a new operatic form known as Wuxi Opera.

The most influential Wuxi Opera was *Meet at the Temple* (*An Tang Xiang Hui*), which was originally a very popular Tanhuang in the Wuxi region during the late Qing Dynasty. The play's heroine, Jin Xiuying, has been betrothed from childhood to Chen Axing, who lives in the same village. Jin and Chen grow up together but whilst Jin's family becomes rich, Chen's family becomes poor. Jin's father attempts to break the marriage contract, but Jin goes to meet Chen in secret.

The lyrics of this Tanhuang focus on the poverty of Chen's family, described through vivid metaphors: "You are the clay Buddha statute that cannot be raised, the rush lamp wick that cannot be straightened, the decayed bean curd that cannot be cooked well, and leather rope that cannot be picked up. You are the cooker that cannot be heated for a hundred days, and the stone mill whose core has decayed for a thousand years. You are a dying person with one last breath, you are a rotten woodcarving."

Tanhuang prevailed in the area around Jiangsu and Zhejiang during the late Qing Dynasty. The local Tanhuang (called Dongxiang tune in the area around Shanghai), grew from a simple singing recital by three to five people, to a more developed performance, requiring acting as well as singing. These performances caught the attention of audiences in tea houses and other venues in Shanghai and nearby towns.

In the tea houses in Shanghai, such performances gradually evolved towards full-scale opera. Tunes were based on the original simple melodies and beats of story-telling Tanhuang tunes. These melodies and rhythms gradually diversified, eventually forming a

The Chuju Opera *Broken Bridge*, based on the folk tale *Legend of White Snake*, is a love story about the white snake and the scholar Xu Xian.

new opera style, Shanghai Opera. Shanghai Operas include *Meet at the Temple*, *A Bi Da Goes Home* (*A Bi Da Hui Niang Jia*), *Lu Yachen*, *Qiuxiang Delivers Tea* (*Qiu Xiang Song Cha*), and *Grinding Soybean to make Bean Curd* (*Mo Dou Fu*).

Shaoxing Opera, which originated in Zhejiang, developed even more rapidly. It emerged from the Tanhuang story telling and singing that had long been popular in Zhejiang's Shengxian County and surrounding rural areas. During the Ming and Qing dynasties performers developed songs and unique performances by changing purely narrative songs into an early form of performance with both singing and story-telling, forming relatively complete performances with a uniform style. These artists excelled at singing well-known stories, many of which were derived from folk narratives such as *Pearl Pagoda* (*Zhen Zhu Ta*), *The Selling of the Wife* (*Mai Po Ji*), and *Selling Charcoal* (*Mai Qing Tan*).

In the Spring Festival of 1906, some performers in Shengxian County staged full operas in Yuhang and Lin'an (towns in Zhejiang), at the request of wealthy families and villagers, marking a significant transition from the simple singing of stories to operatic stage performances. These groups were called *didu* troupes because rather than using orchestral instruments, they used a drum and a pair of rosewood boards to produce the sound of *didu*. From the performances of these *didu* troupes, Shaoxing Opera emerged.

In the Spring Festival of 1938, Yao Shuijuan (1916–1976) led her all female Shaoxing Opera troupe to Shanghai, marking a new and important chapter in the history of Shaoxing Opera. Although female, Yao was good at playing male roles. At the time, all-female Shaoxing Opera troupes were common, and through professional training of female performers developed a unique aesthetic which won over numerous audiences in Jiangsu and Zhejiang.

All-female Shaoxing Opera is known for its gentle tunes and rhythms that convey sadness and pathos. It portrays the customs of people in Shanghai while retaining those from the villages, through a clear and elegant folk singing style. Shaoxing Opera encompassed a large number of operas about everyday issues which were relevant to people migrating from different regions of China to Shanghai.

The "feminine" tune pattern and musical style of Shaoxing Opera evoked the beauty of the landscapes south of the Yangtze River. Its femininity was further emphasized by female performers taking the male roles. It is well able to show the emotional turns and twists of a beautiful love story and the sadness of a miserable life tragedy.

In Shaoxing Opera performances, female performers who performed young male roles created a unique artistic phenomenon. Following on from Yao Shuijuan, Yin Guifang (1919–2000) was another actress famed for her portrayal of young males. In traditional operas such as *He Wenxiu* or *Prince of the Desert* (*Sha Mo Wang Zi*) (which was adapted from the US film *Cabin in the Sky*), Yin Guifang established her position as the leading actress of Shaoxing Opera.

He Wenxiu is a traditional Cantonese Opera. A scholar named He Wenxiu is victimized by a treacherous feudal official named Yan Song

The Shaoxing Opera *Fortune-Telling from He Wenxiu.*

Dream of the Red Chamber, a classical Shaoxing Opera.

and as a result, He's entire family suffers. He escapes to make a living by singing opera. Wang Lanying, a girl from a rich family, is attracted by He's talent and learns of his unfortunate experiences. The two meet in private and are married, but their union is not accepted by Wang's family so the couple flee to Haining. Unexpectedly, Zhang Tang, a rich local man, makes a false charge against them and the two are forced to separate. He flees again, while Wang is saved by Aunt Yang, a tea house owner. Once He has escaped for a second time, he returns to his wife's residence where she is holding a memorial ceremony to mark their third year apart. As Zhang Tang is still present, He fears being discovered, so he dresses up as a fortune teller and visits his wife. Wang asks the fortune-teller to tell the fortune of her husband. He, holding an abacus, is outwardly calm but inwardly his emotions rise, "Specific birthday is distinct. Wenxiu will tell his own fortune. I cannot tell the fortune of others, but I can tell you mine accurately."

Both Yao Shuijuan and Yin Guifang pioneered women's Shaoxing Opera. Audiences came to accept all-female Shaoxing Opera and the style rapidly became the most popular in the city. Decades later, Shaoxing Opera continues to be performed all over the country, and

Yin Guifang, known as the Empress of Shaoxing Opera, directs a rehearsal.

remains a popular theatrical form in a wide range of regions.

From the late nineteenth century to the early twentieth century, performing artists in Hebei turned their rudimentary singing performances into Pingju Opera. Lianhualao and Yangge, also known as *laozi* and *bengbeng*, were folk songs and dances. *Laozi* troupes consisted of seven or eight actors. The Qing government had strict control over *laozi*, so the troupes would often select the tea houses in the concession or other uncontrolled areas to perform in, such as outdoor enclosures.

A Portrait of Cheng Zhaocai.

The Pingju Opera *Third Sister Yang Goes to Court*. Xin Fengxia plays the role of the Third Sister Yang.

Their performances covered increasingly rich plots and the genre also changed in style. In turn, character roles, costume and make-up diversified; from clowns with pigtails with simple colored make up, *Little Miss Chatterbox* (*Xiao Gu Xian*) and *Picking Plum Branches* (*Shi Mei Zhi*) became independent and could be performed with full make-up. While simple and rough, these performances are highly entertaining and are therefore are very popular.

In 1909, the nascent Pingju Opera entered Tangshan, a central city in the eastern part of Hebei. It thrived in the highly commercialized environment of the city. Early Pingju Opera artists, Wang Fengting and Cheng Zhaocai (1874–1929) performed operas such as *Wonders of the Present and the Past* (*Jin Gu Chuan Qi*) and *Flower is a Go-between* (*Hua Wei Mei*), *Widow Named Ma Sets up a Store* (*Ma Gua Fu Kai Dian*), and *Winning the Beauty Queen* (*Zhan Hua Kui*). Through successful performances of these operas, the quality of Pingju Opera improved substantially as performers amended *lianhualao's* character roles, tune patterns, movement and accompaniment.

Cheng Zhaocai played a vital role in the development of Pingju Opera. He was one of the key figures in the process of transforming Pingju Opera from *lianhualao* to Tangshan *laozi*. Cheng completed no less than ninety Pingju Operas. *Third Sister Yang Goes to Court* (*Yang San Jie Gao Zhuang*), is one of the most outstanding and since its debut in 1919, the opera has constantly been in production.

The opera was based on a real event that happened in Luanxian County, Hebei, in 1918. Yang, a peasant girl who is the third sister in her family, accuses her brother-in-law's family of killing her second elder sister. She goes to the county government office to complain, but the officials have been bribed. Yang then goes to the Tianjin Higher Procuratorial Department to appeal and the case is finally heard by the newly appointed director general. Her sister's coffin is opened, the body inspected and the truth discovered. The murderer is then executed. The story portrays the struggle of a woman at the lowest level of the society who fights against the tyranny of the rich and powerful. Yang's perseverance inspired numerous audiences.

The predecessors of Chuju Opera, Shaoxing Opera and Pingju Opera can be divided into two categories. The first category includes Flower-Drum Opera, Lantern Opera, Tea-Picking Opera and *Yangge*, forms evolved from folk songs and dances. They employed simple performing methods to convey stories of mutual longing, flirtation and love between men and women. Occasionally there were comedies and satires on greediness, meanness and laziness. From simple storytelling through singing, performances diversified to include acting. These small plays formed the original basis of the narrative traditions of various new operas. In the second category are the operas derived from *lianhualao, tanhuang,* and *daoqing,* popular from the south to the north. There is a clear distinction between these operas and traditional singing and dancing, but they maintain the tradition of telling long stories.

From the beginning of the Tang and Song dynasties, the style blossomed as it transitioned from temples to popular folk performances.

In just a few decades, various regions around China witnessed the emergence of Huangmei Opera, Hunan Flower-Drum Opera, Jiangxi Tea-Picking Opera, Yunnan Lantern Opera, and Shandong Lüju Opera, as well as new operas transformed from *yangge* and *daoqing* in the north of China, which, to varying degrees, absorbed

Yangliuqing New Year Picture of Shibuxian. Shibuxian was a folk form popular in Beijing, Tianjin, and Hebei during the Qing Dynasty. Folk tales were accompanied by ten percussion instruments including gongs, drums, cymbals and reverse cymbals.

the advantages of such big operas as Kunqu Opera, high-pitched tunes, and *luantan*, and whose plays, music and performance became diversified. At the same time, they continued to maintain the characteristics of interesting and humorous lyrics and performance styles and embody the wisdom and imagination of the folk performances from which they developed. After the 1920s, their rise was unstoppable.

Modern Stage Plays

In the late nineteenth century, as cultural exchanges between China and the western world increased, European dramas were introduced into China. Shanghai, the first commercial port in China, was the birthplace of modern Chinese drama. In the mid-nineteenth century, the presence of an increasing number of expatriates from various western countries in Shanghai prompted the development of Western drama in China. Westerners built and ran churches and schools which created opportunities for drama to develop.

Shanghai's first drama performance occurred in 1850 following the establishment of an amateur dramatic society in the British concession. The Amateur Dramatic Club of Shanghai (ADC) was set up by Western expatriates living in Shanghai in 1866 to stage classic Western plays for expatriate audiences. In 1874, the building of Shanghai Lyceum Theatre was completed, becoming the permanent venue for ADC productions in the concession.

Later, concession mission schools such as the French-run College St. Ignace organized students to produce religious plays every year. The form of these performances was different from traditional Chinese operas and was the first contact that Chinese people (the students) had with drama.

Liturgical dramas encouraged mission school students' interest in theatre and in 1889, the students of St John's College, a mission school in Shanghai, performed *A Shameful Story About Officialdom* (*Guan Chang Chou Shi*), the first modern Chinese play. In 1900, Shanghai Nanyang College students staged *Six Gentlemen* (*Liu Jun Zi*), *On the Nation* (*Jing Guo Mei Tan*) and *Boxer Uprising* (*Yi He Tuan*)—three modern dramas based on contemporary events.

Student dramas flourished in early twentieth-century Shanghai. Nankai College in the north set up a student troupe and created and performed *New Village Head* (*Xin Cun Zheng*) and *One Yuan* (*Yi Yuan Qian*). In 1903, the Yucai School performed *Zhang Wenxiang Assassinates Ma Xinyi* (*Zhang Wen Xiang Ci Ma*). In the play, Ma Xinyi, governor general of Jiangsu and Jiangxi and a provincial tycoon, is killed by the assassin Zhang Wenxiang. The case shocks the court and the people. The intrigue, especially the identity of the assassin Zhang Wenxiang, stimulates people's imagination. Rumors spread. Even before the case was concluded, the Shanghai Opera House had already created a new play, interpreting the assassination story as a heroic one. The play performed by the Yucai School was based on this story.

Black Slaves' Appeal to Heaven, performed by the Chunyang Society in 1907.

Dramas performed by school students began to be produced beyond the confines of the schools themselves. In 1905, the students of Shanghai Minli High School began to stage performances in the city. Wang Zhongsheng (1880–1911) recruited some of the students to perform *Black Slaves' Appeal to Heaven* (*Hei Nu Yu Tian Lu*), adapted from the famous American novel *Uncle Tom's Cabin*. The new company was called the Chunyang Society and became the first professional modern drama troupe in China.

The Chunyang Society performed many new plays such as *New Camellia* (*Xin Cha Hua*), adapted from *The Lady of the Camellias* by French writer Alexandre Dumas, *A Flower in a Sea of Sins* (*Nie Hai Hua*), *Exposure of Officialdom* (*Guan Chang Xian Xing Ji*), *Qiu Jin* and *Xu Xilin*. All were adapted from popular novels.

Such modern dramas were popular amongst educated people eager to expand their learning. Troupes and drama societies dedicated to performing modern dramas appeared and vanished quickly. Shanghai's modern drama troupes often performed in surrounding cities such as Wuxi, Suzhou, Nanjing, Wuhu and Changzhou, and even performed as far as Wuhan, Beijing and

The modern opera *Bad Family*, performed by the Xinmin Society in 1913.

Tianjin, so that Shanghai modern drama extended its influence to other regions.

Zheng Zhengqiu (1888–1935) was an important manager in Shanghai's modern drama scene during the early stages of the Republic of China, and he made an outstanding contribution to the development of modern dramas. He wrote *Bad Family* (*E Jia Ting*), a play based on the political climate of the time, which was performed by the Minming Society, who went on to produce plays such as the *Empress Dowager* (*Xi Tai Hou*) and *Laugh in the Sleeve* (*San Xiao Yin Yuan*).

Performances of these modern dramas broke the dominance of traditional operas, enabling Chinese audiences to experience new kinds of theatre. Encouraged by early successes, Zheng Zhengqiu created the Xinmin Society, adapting popular Peking Operas such as *The Hate* (*Hen Hai*), *The Tablet of Blood and Tears* (*Xue Lei Bei*), *Lotus Nunnery* (*Lian Hua An*) and *The Case of the Murderous Son* (*Sha Zi Bao*) into modern plays.

Modern dramas gradually incorporated aspects of contemporary Chinese life in their themes, enriching the urban

Thunderstorm.

cultural sphere. The Chinese Drama Society, set up with the support of Chen Dabei (1887–1944) in 1922, brought together forty-eight member organizations across the country (most of which were school drama societies), including student drama societies at Beijing's Tsinghua University, the Beijing Higher Normal College, and the Beijing Women's Higher Normal College.

Chen, who had studied in France in his youth, was a teacher at a mission school in Suzhou. Known for playing No.1 Tragic Female Role in early modern dramas, he instead advocated non-professional dramas.

A more significant shift was begun by Hong Shen (1894–1955), Xiong Foxi (1900–1965) and Yu Shangyuan (1897–1970), who returned to China after studying in Europe to play a critical role in the development of modern dramas in the 1920s. They were the first Chinese opera artists to receive Western dramatic training and through their efforts, the styles, methods and theoretical foundations of Western drama took root in China.

In 1933, Tang Huaiqiu (1898–1954) set up the Travelling Drama Troupe of China in Shanghai. The troupe, which was active for fourteen years, was the first professional theatre to be supported solely through the income generated by ticket sales.

Comic plays were an unexpected product of the development of modern dramas. These bawdy comedies took the form of modern dramas, but were performed in the Shanghai dialect.

Following its establishment, the Travelling Drama Troupe of China went on tour to various cities with plays such as the incredibly popular *Thunderstorm (Lei Yu)* by the famous Chinese playwright Cao Yu.

Cao Yu (1910–1996) became interested in theatre whilst at school. Influenced by Zhang Boling (1876–1951), the President of Nankai College, and his younger brother Zhang Pengchun (1892–1957), Cao joined the Nankai Modern Drama Troupe, playing the hero the play *Nora* and co-writing *The New Head of the Village* with Zhang Pengchun. The two also collaborated on the translation of Moliere's famous play *The Miser,* which they adapted into a three-act play called *Crazy for Money (Cai Kuang)*, in which Cao played the hero.

From the outset Cao Yu was guided and directed by Zhang Pengchun, a scholar with an in-depth understanding of European and US dramas, and indeed the thematic and stylistic features of Cao's initial script of *Thunderstorm* were directly influenced by European and American trends. Cao Yu completed *Thunderstorm*, which took him five years to write, just before his graduation from college in 1933. His four-act stage play was published the following year and quickly gained critical acclaim. Despite being his first work, it is

Cao Yu.

the play for which he is most famous. In 1936 and 1937, yet to reach the age of thirty, Cao Yu had a further two plays published; *Sunrise (Ri Chu)* and *Wilderness (Yuan Ye)*. Cao Yu's three masterpieces became the unsurpassable classics of modern drama which continue to influence playwrights today.

In modern drama, Chinese opera gained a new theatrical form which enabled it to diversify and expand. For 100 years, modern stage plays have gradually been assimilated into Chinese culture, through the fusion of Western forms with Chinese aesthetics. Cao Yu allowed drama to embody enduring values in the field of Chinese literature and the literary status of plays, just like ancient Yuan *zaju* and Ming and Qing *chuanqi*, is recognized by audiences.

Global Presence

The New Theatres

Chinese Opera faced many uncertainties as a result of increasing contact between China and the outside world from the mid-nineteenth century onwards. Inevitably, it underwent huge changes in form as it was subjected to the overwhelming impact of the global wave of modernization and industrialization.

Owing to the popularity of Peking Opera during the Qing Dynasty, opera houses, known as tea houses, began to spring up in cities and towns all over China, having previously only been found in Peking. However, Peking Opera did not totally dominate as local residents also remained faithful to their local styles. From the beginning of twentieth century the emergence of new theatres changed these beloved opera houses. In 1908, the Shanghai New Theatre was completed. It did not take long for other theatres to model themselves on the New Theatre and the style swept across the country in a few years.

The Shanghai Tianchan Theatre, built in 1925 for the performance of Peking Opera. It had more than 3,400 seats and many well-known actors of Peking Opera, such as Mei Lanfang, Xun Huisheng, Ma Lianliang, Gai Jiaotian and Yu Zhenfei, performed on its stage.

In 1907, brothers Xia Yueshan (1868–1924) and Xia Yuerun (1878–1931), owners of the Dangui Tea House, along with Peking Opera artist Pan Yueqiao (1869–1928) and a group of Chinese landowners and merchants, launched and funded an expensive new enterprise. Located on the Huangpu River, the Shanghai New Theatre was completely different from traditional opera houses and was the first Western-style theatre to be built in China for the performance of Chinese operas. Its architectural style was influenced by Western theatres as the Xia brothers had traveled abroad to study, visiting Japan and Europe.

The Shanghai Lyceum Theatre, built in 1931. It was mainly used for the performance of modern dramas and concerts.

The New Theatre was a large oval, where the audience was seated on three levels. The ground floor was called the hall, the second level was for VIPs and the third for ordinary people.

An interior view of the Lyceum Theatre.

Thus, the capacity of the theatre was greatly enlarged and sight-lines were improved. All spectators faced the stage, the seating was raked, and side tables (which had been used for tea and refreshments) were removed, highlighting the primary aim of the New Theatre—that the audiences' enjoyment of the show was paramount.

The New Theatre featured an innovative, semi-circular stage with a small apron, which faced the audience on three sides. It was an amalgamation of Eastern and Western designs: The stage of traditional Chinese teahouse opera was a thrust stage with a back-drop, whereas in the West at that time, proscenium arch theatres with enclosed box sets (where the audience all faced the same way) predominated.

For performers, different stage layouts required different performing techniques. In tea houses, performers had to take account of audiences on three sides, whereas in proscenium arch theatres, actors only had to focus on the front. Therefore, although the New Theatre adopted Western architectural styles, the configuration of the stage took into consideration the habits of Chinese audiences. Moreover, the New Theatre improved sight-lines by removing two large pillars usually found downstage on traditional teahouse stages.

The much bigger stage of the New Theatre allowed performers to enjoy a larger acting space and use more props, and increasingly complex backdrops gradually became an important element of opera performances, completely overturning Chinese theatrical tradition. The birth of this Western-style New Theatre gave rise to the first generation of set designers in China. Zhang Yuguang (1885–1968) was invited to become the stage director at the New Theatre. He designed numerous sets for the New Theatre and is regarded as the founder of set design in Chinese opera.

Within a few years of the establishment of the New Theatre, similar theatres had sprung up throughout Shanghai. As competition in the performing market became increasingly fierce towards the end of the nineteenth century, many new opera forms gradually emerged, the most significant of which was the "serialized drama" of Peking Opera.

Once Peking Opera had entered Shanghai and proliferated, serialized dramas provided a new way of attracting the local audience. At the turn of the century, the Tianxian Tea House created several successful serialized dramas. The popular play *The Miser (Tie Gong Ji)* was based on historical events. Jiangnan Prefect Xiang Rong and the betrayed Taiping general Zhang Jiaxiang attack Nanjing with the Qing army and fight with the Taiping troops, during the Taiping Heavenly Kingdom Period (also known as the Taiping Rebellion).*The Miser*, which has twelve episodes, was written and performed by Wang Hongshou (1850–1925), an actor in the Tianxian Tea House, with Zhao Songshou as the drummer.

The Miser embodied many characteristic elements of Shanghai Peking Opera. It was dynamic, lively and thrilling, with a simple theme which clearly articulated right from wrong. Colorful lighting illuminated the actors and actresses who performed with real swords, spears and guns, and used stunts like jumping through a ring of fire, ushering in a new style of acrobatic fighting. *The Miser* became the most beloved Peking Opera in Shanghai.

From the prevalence of Kunqu to the more action-based productions of Peking Opera, artistic techniques - singing, speaking, acting and fighting - became more important, whilst plot lines were somewhat neglected. However, the flourishing of local dramas all over the country, and serialized dramas in Shanghai, saved Chinese opera from decline.

During the period of the Republic of China, operas were mainly performed in cities and were susceptible to the effects of market forces. At that time, Cantonese Opera was regarded as the most commercial form of drama.

Having experienced a recovery at the end of the Qing Dynasty, Cantonese Opera entered a golden age during the Republic. The emergence of new style theatres led to an explosion of new

Xue Juexian in *Bai Jinlong*.

plays, which were mainly watched by ordinary workers whose interests and tastes also influenced its evolution.

In Cantonese Opera, singing and fighting were very important and performers tended to dress in dazzling and outlandish costumes. Yet the greatest change was in the kinds of plays that were performed. From the 1920s to the 1930s, thousands of new plays were written and the traditional themes of Cantonese Opera were changed.

Although similar to Han Opera and Peking Opera, Cantonese Opera differed in its emphasis on family sagas and love stories. An example is the play *Bai Jinlong*, adapted from an American movie, which is a love story about Bai Jinlong, the son of a rich man, and Zhang Yuniang, a girl from a declining noble family. Bai pretends to be a servant in Zhang's house and saves Zhang's valuable jewelry in order to win her favor. After she is seized by two local pimps, Bai disguises himself as a Western woman and rescues Zhang. The plays ends with the couple's marriage. The play's theme, compact layout and the famous actor Xue Juexian (1904–1956), contributed to its nine-month run, and it broke box-office records. As love stories became common in theatres, *dan* (the female role) gradually rose to be as important as *sheng* (the male role).

Being Conferred Prime Minister by Six Kingdoms, the most famous serial Cantonese Opera.

In the late Qing Dynasty, these opulent operatic forms were performed in rural areas in Guangdong and Guangxi Provinces, where theatrical companies comprising about 160 people would perform for a period of five days. Shows would start in the afternoon and conclude at nine or ten o'clock the next morning. Each time a troupe arrived in a new place it generated great excitement amongst the locals.

Efficient organization, lavish spending and strict performing regulations won the support of rich elites. However, such performances were banned in urban theatres and after the political and social structures that underpinned the traveling companies collapsed, commercial profit became the most direct and effective driver of changes in the performance system.

One important example was the ten-year competition between the Jue Xiansheng Troupe, led by Xue Juexian, and the Taiping Troupe, led by Ma Shizeng (1900–1964), a rivalry which was the driving force of Cantonese Opera from the mid-to late period of the Republic. It was a rivalry which inspired performers, playwrights and directors in Guangzhou and Hong Kong. As a result, Cantonese Opera became predominant in Southeast Asia and spread globally as people from Lingnan traveled abroad.

Throughout the twenties and thirties, various new musical instruments, including western ones, started appearing in Cantonese Opera, leading to significant changes in the music used. During the Qing Dynasty, the main musical instruments were the *erxian* (a two-string fiddle) and the *yueqin* (a plucked lute with a wooden body, a short fretted neck, and four strings tuned in pairs), and the gong, drum and cymbal. During the period of the Republic, the *erhu* (Chinese two-string violin) became the most popular instrument, replacing the two-string fiddle. At the same time, the *qinqin* (a plucked lute with a wooden body and fretted neck) took the place of *yueqin*. Western musical instruments that were frequently used include the violin and saxophone, whilst the guitar, jazz drum and electric guitar also sometimes featured.

The changes in Cantonese Opera during the first half of the twentieth century were, to a large extent, influenced by Western popular art and American movies. It was not until the 1950s that Cantonese Opera sought to return to the tradition and charm of its origins.

The Global Success of Mei Lanfang

The status and influence of Peking Opera made rapid strides during the period of the Republic of China. After the death of Tan Xinpei, gradually the people who came to be seen as the most distinguished practitioners were Yu Shuyan (1890–1943), Yang Xiaolou (1877–1938) and Mei Lanfang (1894–1961).

Yu Shuyan demonstrated great self-discipline in studying Tan Xinpei's artistic performances despite the social unrest of the early stages of the Republic. By attending all Tan's live shows, Yu learnt Tan's tunes, words and gestures by heart. After Tan Xinpei's death, Yu Shuyan continued, although less directly, to learn from him. Concentrating on his studies for over ten years, Yu finally managed to propel Tan's art into a new realm, keeping its artistic essence, but eliminating the shortcomings of Tan's singing.

Yu remained dedicated to pure art in the face of increasing commercialization. He was highly disciplined and polished all his performances to perfection. Yu's greatest contribution was the perfection of Peking Opera performances, which is why he is recognized as a great master.

Mei Lanfang was the most influential actor of the Republic of China. Born to a family of Peking Opera performers in Beijing, he performed in public for the first time at the age of ten, at the Guanghe Theatre, in a piece called The Fairy Couple (Tian Xian Pei). Following this, Mei Lanfang's fame grew. He gave his first professional performance in Shanghai in 1913, and his productions soon dominated the vast area south of the Yangtze River. One year later, he returned to Shanghai and performed in several famous traditional plays including *The Drunken Concubine* (*Gui Fei Zui Jiu*) for thirty-four successive days. By studying the different styles and roles of Peking Operas including *qingyi*, *huadan* and *daomadan*, Mei Lanfang developed his own unique style of singing, speaking and dressing. His singing, in particular, won him a tremendous reputation and contributed to the foundation of the School of Mei. In 1927, when a competition to decide the best *dan* (female role) performers in China was organized by the Shuntian Times, Mei Lanfang, already famous for his artistic knowledge, beautiful voice and makeup, won the position of one

Yu Shuyan plays the role of Huang Zhong in *The Battle of Dingjunshan*.

The "Four Famous Dan Actors" in 1949. From left to right: Xun Huisheng, Mei Lanfang, Shang Xiaoyun and Cheng Yanqiu.

of the "Four Famous Dan Actors" along with Cheng Yanqiu (1904–1958), Shang Xiaoyun (1900–1976) and Xun Huisheng (1900–1968).

Mei Lanfang was an idol of his time. But Mei Lanfang's more significant contribution was his successive visits to Japan, the US and the Soviet Union, presenting the attractions of Chinese traditional operas to the world.

In December 1929, Mei Lanfang and his troupe traveled to the US. On February 16, 1930, he officially launched his show at the 49th Street Theatre on Broadway. Recognizing that American audiences would have little knowledge of Chinese traditional operas, Mei planned accordingly and tried to interest American spectators by printing beautiful advertising materials as well as books on Chinese opera containing detailed pictures and illustrations. Mei Lanfang asked Zhang Pengchun, who was a drama expert who had studied in America, to be the master of ceremonies. The repertoire and performance patterns were also adjusted to suit the tastes of the new audience and before each show, Zhang Pengchun would give the audience a simple introduction to the opera. During his six-month visit to the US, Mei Lanfang acted in many cities, including New York, Chicago, San Francisco, Los Angeles and Honolulu.

Although Chinese opera performances in the US can be traced back to the earliest Chinese immigrant workers, Mei Lanfang's visit marked the introduction of traditional Chinese opera into American culture as Mei's artistic performances caught the attention of the most influential operatic scholars and critics, as well as the mainstream media. Mei Lanfang was

Male Dan

Male *dan* refers to the male actors who perform female roles in traditional Chinese theatre. Such acting was common in Peking Opera and other kinds of operas during the Qing Dynasty. Love stories usually required intimate scenes but the Qing governments strictly prohibited female performers from acting with male actors, because it was regarded as a violation of social morals. Therefore, with women excluded from private troupes which performed in the palaces of Qing officials, men played every character in a drama. That is how male *dan* came into being. Female performers existed, too, but they acted in troupes where all the members were women. These restrictions were gradually eliminated after 1921. By strict and systematic training, a good male *dan* could skillfully use his physiological features to present the attitude, gestures and elegant beauty of the female figures in plays.

Mei Lanfang and Yang Xiaolou perform in *Farewell My Concubine* in 1922. Yang enjoyed the title of "Master of Wusheng," a male martial arts role in Peking Opera.

During his visit to the US, Mei Lanfang met Charlie Chaplin.

subsequently awarded honorary doctorates by Pomona College and the University of Southern California.

Invited by the International Culture Exchange Association of the Soviet Union, Mei Lanfang visited Russia to perform with his troupe in 1935. The Chinese delegation included practitioners such as Zhang Pengchun and Yu Shangyuan, opera scholars with a sound understanding of both oriental and occidental style, whilst the Russian delegation was led by the famous theatre practitioner Stanislavski. Other committee members included Danchenko, Meyerhold, Eisenstein and other world-class luminaries. Mei Lanfang put on a number of performances in Moscow and

During his visit to the US, Mei Lanfang meets with the Governor of Honolulu.

Leningrad, to which large audiences, including performers and students, thronged.

His performances deeply impressed foreign opera practitioners. Meyerhold, a famous director, even commented that "After seeing how Mei Lanfang uses his hands in his operas, the only

Mei Lanfang visits the Soviet Union in 1935.

Mei Lanfang receives French guests at his house in Beijing.

thing Russian performers can do is to cut their own hands off."
Before Mei left Moscow, a round-table conference was arranged
by the USSR International Culture Exchange Association. Mei
Lanfang, Zhang Pengchun and Yu Shangyuan attended along
with Stanislavski, Danchenko, Meyerhold and Eisenstein, as well
as famous musicians and dancers from the Soviet Union. They
all spoke extremely highly of Mei. Bertolt Brecht, the famous and
influential German practitioner, who happened to be in the USSR
at this time, watched Mei Lanfang's performance and was deeply
moved. In his article "Alienation Effects in Chinese Acting" he
proposed a new theory of opera and set out a unique form of
opera performance by examining Mei Lanfang's performance
in plays like *The Fisherman's Revenge* (*Da Yu Sha Jia*). Following
his performances in the Soviet Union, Mei Lanfang continued to
perform in Europe, where he studied foreign plays.

His visit to the Soviet Union was more culturally significant than
that of any other Chinese opera performer because his profound
discussions with well-known opera performers from the USSR and
Eastern Europe represented the first face-to-face dialogue between
the USSR and China about each country's idea of opera.

During the 1980s such exchanges become more frequent and intensive and the footprints of Chinese opera can now be found all over Europe. In turn, in the last hundred years, Western operas, from the classic to the post-modernist, have all been performed China, influencing modern Chinese dramatists.

Improvements to Traditional Opera and Model Opera

On October 1, 1949, the People's Republic of China was founded. Changes in the social system also resulted in significant changes to plays. The new government valued traditional operas highly and asked the Ministry of Culture to set up a specialized department for drama improvement. Relevant departments were also set up in local government and officials were sent to theatrical companies to improve operas in three ways: Improving the performers, the staging and the operas.

In September 1949, four artists of traditional opera were invited to the first plenary session of the Chinese People's Political Consultative Conference. They were Mei Lanfang, Zhou Xinfang

(1895–1975), Cheng Yanqiu and Yuan Xuefen. In 1954, during the first National People's Congress, seven opera performers were elected as deputies to the NPC: Peking Opera artists Mei Lanfang, Zhou Xinfang and Cheng Yanqiu, Shaoxing Opera artist Yuan Xuefen, Yu Opera artist Chang Xiangyu (1923–2004), Chuan Opera artist Chen Shufang (1924–1996) and Lüju Opera artist Lang Xianfen. As a result, they were able to participate directly in national political affairs, reflecting the significant enhancement of the social status of opera performers. In local regions, many opera artists became deputies and committee members of the local NPC and CPPCC.

For thousands of years, actors in China had been considered to be vagabonds. Even after the Yuan Dynasty, when opera scripts became more accepted as literary styles, opera performers were still subject to all kinds of discrimination. Only after the founding of the new China in 1949 were actors and actresses finally able to climb from their low position in society and receive political honors, revealing the new government' s recognition of their value and the social status they deserved.

In the meantime, there were gradual improvements in the ownership of opera troupes, (most of which had been privately owned), when they became republic troupes. The actors and actresses initially shared joint ownership but eventually troupes were nationalized and guided by, or directly affiliated to, the government. Improvements to civic structures in cities also included improvements to theatrical performances. Since the Song Dynasty, opera performances had been commercialized. These changes went a long way towards strengthening theatre's educational functions, putting less emphasis on profit, which would play a less significant role over time. As a result, the original theatre business model was effectively abolished. Improvements also included a series of measures named "stage purification," which included dismissing prop managers, not allowing performers to drink tea while acting and officially removing tea and candy shops from theatres.

Artists and writers attend the First Session of the National People's Congress of China in 1954.
In this photo are Yuan Xuefen, Cheng Yanqiu, Chang Xiangyu, Zhou Xinfang and Mei Lanfang.

Performers taking part in the First National Chinese Opera Festival in 1952.

The Shaoxing Opera *Butterfly Lovers*.

These measures changed the habits that had been formed during the late Qing Dynasty, when opera was played in tea houses, resulting in the disappearance of many distinctive customs from traditional theatres. The ultimate goal was to highlight the artistic aspects of the productions.

The core of the opera improvement campaign lay in reforming a large number of traditional plays. Guided by government-appointed committees, dozens of plays were identified as "model plays" and were performed during the First National Chinese Opera Festival held by the Ministry of Culture in 1952. Attended by over 1,600 performers from 37 troupes and covering 23 different styles of opera and most of the provinces, it was considered the first national opera show in Chinese history. During the festival, 87 plays were performed, including 63 traditional ones, 11 new historical plays and 8 modern ones.

The measures taken by authorities were clearly visible in the national opera festival, during which the most noteworthy plays were three versions of *The Butterfly Lovers* (*Liang Shan Bo Yu Zhu Ying Tai*)—the Shaoxing Opera version, the Peking Opera version and the Chuan Opera version—and the Peking Opera and Shaoxing Opera versions of *The Tale of the White Snake* (*Bai She Zhuan*).

The Shaoxing Opera version of *The Butterfly Lovers* was based on the tragedy of Liang and Zhu (*Liang Zhu Ai Shi*) and was performed by Yuan Xuefen. Regarded as a model play, it had a high status in government circles even before the national opera festival. *The Butterfly Lovers* is based on a well-known folk tale, telling a sad love story of Zhu Yingtai, the only child of a rich family in Shangyu, Zhejiang. She loves reading, but can only pursue her studies disguised as a man because women did not have the right to receive education at the time. On her way to Hangzhou in search of a better education, she meets Liang Shanbo, who has the same aim. The two become sworn brothers and forge a deep friendship during three years of study at the end of which Zhu returns home and Liang insists on seeing Zhu off. Distressed at their impending departure, Zhu frequently hints to Liang, through various metaphors, that she is a woman and that she is determined to be with him for all eternity. Unfortunately Liang is a bookworm and does not get the message. Months later, he finally discovers Zhu is a woman and happily goes to Zhu's family to propose, but her father has already arranged for her to marry Ma Wencai, the son of a local official.

The Shaoxing Opera *Butterfly Lovers*, performed by the Zhejiang Xiaobaihua Shaoxing Opera Troupe. The role of Liang Shanbo is played by Mao Weitao.

Liang and Zhu meet in a pavilion in Zhu's house, but can only cry at the ironic circumstances set by fate. Liang is desperate and heartbroken. His health gradually deteriorates until he becomes seriously ill and dies. Zhu Yingtai falls into great despair and sadness after hearing the news. On her wedding day, she insists on carrying a compass during the procession, which allows her to visit Liang's grave first. When she approaches the grave, mysterious whirlwinds and thunders suddenly occur, the tomb opens and Zhu throws herself into the grave to join Liang Shanbo. At exactly that moment, two beautiful butterflies emerge from the grave, dancing together, said to be the spirits of the couple which cannot be separated, even after death. Over the decades, many different versions of the story have appeared.

The Shaoxing Opera *The Butterfly Lovers* is the best known version in China. Classic scenes, such as "Eighteen Mile Farewell," which describes how Liang Shanbo sees Zhu Yingtai off, and "Meeting in the Pavilion," when Liang goes to propose, are the scenes most enjoyed by audiences.

The opera is typical of the "opera improvement" campaign. It was made into a color movie and received great acclaim in Europe, especially in Eastern European countries. This great opera classic, enriched by numerous performers over thousands of years and repeatedly polished by multiple authors, has gradually moved towards perfection. It has been endowed with even more cultural significance after careful adaptations in the 1950s.

Similar cases can be found all over the country. Most traditional operas could not be performed during the "model play" period as they did not fit the requirements of the ideology. Still, the improvement period had a positive impact by making the plays more sophisticated.

The artistic career of Mei Lanfang demonstrates the huge impact of "opera improvement" from another prospective. Following the tremendous success of his visit to the US and the Soviet Union, Mei Lanfang started to emphasize the classical features of his acting

Mei Lanfang plays the role of Mu Guiying in *Mu Guiying Taking Command*.

and performed plays in which he could use his knowledge of Kunqu Opera, which is known for its delicacy.

The eight most prestigious of these plays are called the *Mei's Eight Plays* and are *The Drunken Concubine* (*Gui Fei Zui Jiu*), *Farewell My Concubine* (*Ba Wang Bie Ji*), *The Surprising Double Meeting* (*Qi Shuang Hui*), *The Returning Love* (*Feng Huan Chao*), *The Cosmos Sword* (*Yu Zhou Feng*), *Hate between Life and Death* (*Sheng Si Hen*), *The Goddess of Luo River* (*Luo Shen*) and *An Interrupted Dream in a Peony Pavilion* (*You Yuan Jing Meng*).

In 1959 Mei Lanfang wrote and acted in the new play *Mu Gui Taking Command* (*Mu Gui Ying Gua Shuai*), the first play he had written since entering middle age. The play was adapted from an opera with the same title and performed by Ma Jinfeng, a well-known Yuju Opera actress.

The play was based on the best parts of *Generals of the Yang Clan* (*Yang Jia Jiang*), an extremely popular story in China. Though only a very few documents can be found in historical records about General Yang Jiye's battle with Jin troops during the Northern Song Dynasty, these records grew into a complicated story with numerous characters and plots, many chapters of which have been adapted into classic Peking Operas and other operas.

Tan Xinpei gained great prestige by playing in *The Tragedy at the Li Ling Monument* (*Tuo Zhao Peng Bei*) and *Hongyang Grave* (*Hong Yang Dong*), which were derived from *Generals of the Yang Clan*.

Mei Lanfang plays the role of Concubine Yang in *Drunk Concubine*.

Also excerpted from this story was *The Fourth Son of the Yang Family Visits His Mother* (*Si Lang Tan Mu*), regarded as one of the most dynamic plays since the birth of Peking Opera, which included the legendary character, Mu Guiying.

Mu Guiying's experience, especially as she takes command to fight the enemy troops in her later years, is described in detail in the play. Several generations of the Yang family sacrifice their lives for their country, leaving only womenfolk. But when the enemies invade again and no other generals can be dispatched, the Yang family becomes the only hope for the court and the country. Facing invasion by the Western Xia Dynasty, the emperor has no choice but to ask the elderly female general Mu Guiying to fight for the country. Mu Guiying intends to refuse, not only because the court has been extremely mean and indifferent to the Yang family but also because, with the exception of Yang Wenguang, the only living son, the other family members have sacrificed their lives for their country. However, taking into account the present national crisis, and persuaded by her grandmother-in-law, she finally decides to take command.

Mei Lanfang was in his sixties in 1959, and this was his first time acting as an old woman. To nobody's surprise, he performed extremely well, especially in the scene of the ceremony where Mu Guiying receives the seal of commander, where his character is instantly transforming from retiring housewife to honored general and sings,

> *Suddenly the sound of drums thunders in my ears, reminding me of previous ambitions. I was so brave and awe-inspiring in the past, leading my people in the front line, with innumerable enemies beheaded under my horse. I will fulfill my duties as long as I am alive; how can I just watch enemies seizing our towns? The king of the enemy is not worth bothering about; my sword could kill millions of his men. If I don't take command, who will? If I don't lead the troops, who will? Quickly, arm me: I will bring my seal, take command and rally the troops!*

Mu Guiying Taking Command was Mei Lanfang's last play. Through this work, he demonstrated that Chinese Opera, after more than eight-hundred years of development, can still achieve excellence, even in a society that was undergoing tremendous change.

Since the 1950s, both the government and artists have been concerned with how to express modern subjects in the style of traditional operas. However, it was not difficult for the newly developed modern play to present modern subjects. The cooperation between playwright Lao She (1899–1966) and director Jiao Juyin (1905–1975) in founding Beijing People's Art Theatre (BPAT) created a new national style for Chinese modern plays.

While directing Lao She's works *Dragon Beard Ditch* (*Long Xu Gou*) and *Teahouse* (*Cha Guan*), Jiao Juyin, who greatly admired the performance system set up by the famous Russian director Stanislavski, tried to make the BPAT a forum for putting Stanislavski' s theories into practice. He required actors and

The first performance of *Teahouse* in 1958.

Teahouse, performed by the Beijing People's Art Theatre.

actresses to form a "mental image" of the characters they would play and to "inhabit" their roles. Jiao Juyin was the first modern Chinese director to create his own style. Under his guidance, the BPAT blossomed.

Within the first ten minutes of *Teahouse*, the playwright introduces dozens of lively characters onstage. The work employs vivid language and a unique structure, based on the playwright's extensive research into teahouse society and history. As a play with a high degree of stylized prose it abandons the traditional principles laid down in textbooks and "shows" the changes of a teahouse in Beijing through three different ages, with no conflict and no story line. Lao She's characters come to life on stage by employing a unique sense of humor that is extremely expressive and embodies Beijing's characteristics.

Traditional dramatists in the 1950s were concerned with ensuring that the new opera preserved its artistic values while achieving propagandist and educational goals. After 1964, as public performances of many traditional operas started to be restricted, writing modern operas became the only choice for dramatists.

Model Opera was the most important style in Chinese opera in the 1960s. It came into being as a traditional opera integrated with modern society.

In 1964, a national festival of modern Peking Opera was held in Beijing, where twenty-nine troupes from institutions directly under the Ministry of Culture in Beijing and Shanghai performed thirty-five plays. It was the biggest national celebration of opera following the National Chinese Opera Festival. Subsequently, local governments began to organize their own joint performances of modern plays. In 1965, another round of modern play performances, based on Peking Opera, were held throughout the country. Opera had become politicized.

Strong political messages, along with the narration of legends were incorporated into the stories of the Model Opera, best illustrated in *Taking Tiger Mountain by Strategy* (*Zhi Qu Wei Hu Shan*), the first Model Opera. The story is based on the novel *Tracks in the Snowy Forest* (*Lin Hai Xue Yuan*), which was based on real incidents in northeast China during the Chinese Civil War. The story takes place in a rebel stronghold. Yang Zirong, the hero, disguises himself as a bandit and spies for the government. War, espionage, danger and suspense make this play extremely dramatic. The stage version by the Shanghai Troupe of Peking Opera won high critical praise and was adopted as a model by troupes all over China when they performed this play. Effective characterization was the priority for dramatists while adapting Model Opera for the stage, because audiences would only be politically

Model Opera
In the 1960s a group of well-designed opera plays emerged whose subjects and styles were endorsed by the authorities. Revised several times, these plays finally became the models for troupes of different kinds of opera all over the country. In May 1967, eight plays were officially named as Model Operas. They were *Taking Tiger Mountain by Strategy* (*Zhi Qu Wei Hu Shan*), *The Legend of the Red Lantern* (*Hong Deng Ji*), *Raid on the White Tiger Regiment* (*Qi Xi Bai Hu Tuan*) and *The Harbor* (*Hai Gang*), *The Red Detachment of Women* (*Hong Se Niang Zi Jun*) and *The White-Haired Girl* (*Bai Mao Nü*) and *Shachipang* (*Sha Jia Bang*). The eight model operas were performed during a festival in Beijing that lasted 37 days and included 218 performances. For a long time, these model plays were the only ones which the authorities permitted to be performed.

influenced when the characters' political attributes won their applause and respect.

The Legend of the Red Lantern (*Hong Deng Ji*), jointly adapted by Weng Ouhong (1909–1994), one of the best playwrights of Peking Opera, and A Jia (1907–1994), one of the best directors, could be regarded as the greatest artistic achievement in Model Opera. In the scene "Telling the Revolutionary History of the Family," the intermingled speaking and singing of Grandma Li is most distinct. Weng Ouhong learnt the form from similar scenes in traditional operas like *Story-Telling with Severed Arm* (*Duan Bi Shuo Shu*) and *Orphan of Zhao*. But since the atmosphere is more intense in *The Legend of the Red Lantern*, this particular technique works better.

Another typical scene is "Attending the Banquet to Debate with Jiu Shan," where there is an arresting, fierce battle of words. This new play had more intense storylines and sharper conflicts between characters than traditional plays such as *The Heroes' Feast* (*Qun Ying Hui*), and the actors and actresses were so idolized by the audience that whenever the play was mentioned at that time, people would talk about the actors and the roles they played: Li Shaochun's Li Yuhe, Liu Changyu's Li Tiemei, Gao Yuqian's Grandma Li and Yuan Shihai's Jiu Shan.

A Model Opera production usually offers a clear distinction between right and wrong. In such plays, characters are divided into two categories, good and bad, which can be recognized by their different performance techniques. For example, good characters will generally strike poses on stage. In the scene "Beating Tiger and Going up the Mountain" from *Taking Tiger Mountain by Strategy*, a series of symbolic actions of Yang Zirong have distinctive patterns. The opera, after absorbing and adapting the patterns from traditional Peking Operas, creates extremely elegant actions of its own.

In the scene "Mental Battle in Shachipang" ("Sha Jia Bang"), the antiphonal singing between A Qingsao, Hu Chuankui and Diao

The Model Opera *Taking Tiger Mountain by Strategy.*

Deyi is regarded as a classic of musical design. The three figures, standing on stage together, not only have solos that express their respective inner feelings, but also sing antiphonal dialogues that show their interaction and conflict.

Emotions expressed in particular sentence patterns make the scene a classic example of Model Opera, the most popular part in *Shachipang.* It highlights the achievements Model Opera made in adapting music. To better present subtle and complicated relations and reveal their respective characters, the three actors employ the similar yet different roles of *dan, sheng* and *jing* of Peking Opera. In particular, the clashing antiphonal singing between A Qingsao and Diao Deyi successfully pushes the characters' emotion to a climax. It is a model of both musicalized drama and dramatized music. The musical achievements of *Taking Tiger Mountain by Strategy* are well recognized. The music adopted in "Beating Tiger and Going up the Mountain" is the most brilliant section of the

The Model Opera *The Legend of the Red Lantern*. Grandma Li tells Li Tiemei about the family's revolutionary history.

play's accompaniment. Later, the introduction of symphony in *Azalea Mountain* (Du Juan Shan) also greatly enriched the musical pattern that can be employed in Peking Opera.

Model Opera did not break completely with the musical styles of traditional Peking Opera. In fact, since the music had to be appropriate to the emotions of the heroic figures, and sympathetic to the rhythm of the time, it renewed and updated traditional music, which is why Model Opera still appeals today.

During the Cultural Revolution (1966–1976) when Model Opera monopolized Chinese opera, a great number of outstanding opera performers all over China were persecuted, as playwriting was affected by political ideology. However, many playwrights of different kinds of opera in various parts of the country stuck with their art, even if they were ordered to write plays with purely political purposes.

The Model Opera *Shachipang.*

Chinese Theatre Looks Forward

At the end of the 1970s, another tremendous change took place. Political reform and the opening-up of China led to a reassessment of Chinese operatic traditions.

Free from censorship, many traditional plays resurfaced. Films including the Shaoxing Opera *Dream of the Red Chamber* (*Hong Lou Meng*) and the Huangmei Opera *Fairy Couple* (*Tian Xian Pei*) soon attracted large audiences back into theatres. Artists enjoyed more freedom and many dramatists transformed their real life experiences into artistic creations, bringing Chinese opera to its most flourishing phase since the 1950s.

The new epoch gave dramatists greater access to the wider world, which resulted in a swarm of new ideas. In the 1980s, a group of playwrights and directors dedicated to "Exploration Plays" drew on modern plays from the West, creating a new theatrical aesthetic. Many of them, led by Lin Zhaohua, became pioneers in modern play exploration.

Built in 1954, the Capital Theatre was the first professional theatre for modern plays in Beijing. Even today, to many modern play fans, it is still their "sacred place."

The Western modernism opened up new opportunities, helping them to break away from the repressive political dogma which had dominated Chinese Opera for decades and strongly restricted artistic development. The play *Absolute Signal* (*Jue Dui Xin Hao*) directed by Lin Zhaohua was the first important Exploration Play, and is recognized as the start of a small theatrical movement in modern Chinese society.

Absolute Signal was shown in the upstairs dining hall of the Beijing People's Art Theatre in November 1982. The script represented something of a breakthrough, as the action happens in the back of a van being driven at night. Xiaohao and his master are on duty as security guards. They meet Heizi and Mifeng who ask them for a ride. Xiaohao and his old friend Heizi both adore Mifeng, creating a love triangle. Heizi, (who intends to steal the goods in the van along with his fellow criminals) the master, who is always on the alert, and careless Xiaohao, form another triangular relationship. It is easy to guess the ending: the conspiracy is wrecked and the two good young people find hope in their love.

Absolute Signal, a play directed by Lin Zhaohua.

All the action takes place in a moving van. On stage the van is represented by a symbolic, enclosed and static structure. Strongly supported by Cao Yu, Director of Beijing People's Art Theatre, *Absolute Signal* was an extraordinary success, although the play had its less successful elements. By being presented in a dining hall, not a typical place for performance, it showed the deliberate intention to rebel against the USSR style grand theatres that had been the overriding influence since the 1950s.

The Bus Stop (Che Zhan), by director Lin Zhaohua, is set at a bus stop in a city suburb on a Saturday evening. Many people intending to take a bus downtown, wait anxiously for a bus that never shows up. Complaining and worried, the people wait in vain as time passes until they have all stood there for ten years and are old, humpbacked and grey-haired. Only then do the people find the stop sign has been out of order for a long time and remember

A scene from *The Bus Stop*.

a silent man, who had waited for the bus for quite a while but had then left quietly and walked to the destination.

The Bus Stop was clearly influenced by Samuel Becket's *Waiting for Godot*, an absurdist masterpiece that combines criticism of the contemporary world with metaphysical questions. Through the depiction of a group of people doggedly waiting for a non-existent bus, it explores people's confusion—a common theme at that time.

The Bus Stop generated enthusiastic acclaim. If *Absolute Signal* exemplifies the beginning of Chinese modern plays, and their breaking away from Ibsenism and the system developed by Stanislavski, then *The Bus Stop* is the result of that breakaway.

The development of traditional operas also contributed to achievements in opera at that time. *Cao Cao and Yang Xiu*, created and performed by the Shanghai Troupe of Peking Opera, is the most well known work of all the new plays of this time. In a competition of new Peking Opera plays, held by the Ministry of Culture in Tianjin in December 1988, *Cao Cao and Yang Xiu* won first place and the title "Best New Peking Opera Play." Later, at China's First Peking Opera Festival, it again received a gold medal.

To Live or to Die, a modern opera of Lin Zhaohua in 2007.

Interestingly, it is not easy to identify the typical dramatic styles of the 1980s in *Cao Cao and Yang Xiu* and it appears not to conform to the innovation of the time. Yet this very non-conformity allowed the playwright, director and main actors to take the time to carefully finish the work. The structure of the play is totally different to tradition. There are many Peking Opera plays whose hero is Cao Cao and they all have relatively straightforward storylines. *Cao Cao and Yang Xiu* is dominated by the rivalry of the two characters, the clashes in their personalities and the ups and downs of their lives. Whilst such ideas are common in Chinese painting, their presence in a play was novel.

Cao Cao and Yang Xiu's distinctive qualities were also apparent in its subject-matter. Following the long period when plays had simply been vehicles for political ideology, *Cao Cao and Yang Xiu* did not aim to convey political messages with historical stories, but aimed at more profound, universal ideas that would resonate in all ages.

Huangmei Opera originated from tea-picking songs in Huangmei County, Hubei, a region which suffered from frequent droughts. Every time a draught came, huge groups people would move to Anqing, Anhui, where they made a living by singing and Huangmei Opera developed.

The Peking Opera, *Cao Cao and Yang Xiu*. Cao Cao is played by Shang Changrong and Yang Xiu is played by Yan Xingpeng.

During the 1950s, owing to the success of many classical plays such as *The Fairy Couple* and *The Cowherd and the Weaving Girl* (*Niu Lang Zhi Nü*), the influence of Huangmei Opera quickly expanded. In 1998 *Huizhou Woman* (*Hui Zhou Nü Ren*), a new play performed by Han Zaifen appeared. *Huizhou Woman* is about an unnamed woman living in a village in Huizhou. She gets married at the age of fifteen and hopes for a beautiful and happy life. But her husband leaves her on the wedding day, because he is not happy with the arranged marriage and is eager for a new life. For thirty-five years, she stays with the family, desperately looking forward to her husband's return. Waiting becomes the only meaning in her life. She could have a new life of her own, but she chooses to wait, rather than walk away from the commitment she made. Thirty-five years later, her husband returns with a new family. She is confused and wants to retreat, not knowing whether there is a way back.

By presenting the heroine of *Huizhou Woman* as nameless, and giving no details of her living conditions and lifestyle, the play calls into question traditional Chinese ethics and morals, but also shows the women's experiences from a female view-point. The

Fairy Couple, a classic Huangmei Opera play.

uniqueness of *Huizhou Woman* also lies its dramatic structure and stage arrangement, where there is no story *per se*, but only a presentation of a state of mind. The gestures and makeup of the heroine, played by Han Zaifen, abandon the aesthetic traditions of Huangmei Opera. Instead, the use of bright colors and eclogue-styled aestheticism on stage, together with a set which represents the old houses of Anhui, created a naturalistic relationship between the fate of the figure and the cultural background in which she had been raised. Therefore, her fate surpasses the level of her individual experience, becoming a metaphor for the fate of poor Chinese women. The play is also an appeal to Chinese opera to adopt international styles of design and performance.

The Liyuan Opera *Mr. Dong and Mrs. Li* (*Dong Sheng Yu Li Shi*) reveals another important trend of Chinese opera in the late twentieth century. After experiencing long-standing doubts and criticizing traditional culture, dramatists began to review the value of Chinese opera and cultural traditions. *Mr. Dong and Mrs. Li* is representative this moment.

Liyuan Opera was created from the Minnan dialect, found in the Fujian region and Taiwan. Classic texts including *Gao Wenju,*

The Huangmei Opera *Huizhou Woman*. Han Zaifen plays the lead role.

Chen San and Wu Niang, have survived since the Song Dynasty. The present version of *Chen San and Wu Niang* is almost the same as the edition published in the forty-fifth year of the reign of Jiajing, Emperor of the Ming Dynasty (1566). Today's Liyuan Opera maintains the role system and performance patterns of Song Yuan Nan Opera, requiring performers to follow strict aesthetic principles. Many musical patterns from the Tang and Song Dynasties have been retained. As during the Tang Dynasty, the lutes are all horizontally played; the *erxian* are derived from *xiqin* in the Jin Dynasty; and the vertical flutes are actually *chiba* of the Tang Dynasty. No other kind of opera being performed today can compare with Liyuan Opera in

A stage photo of the Liyuan Opera *Mr. Dong and Mrs. Li.*

its complete preservation of the performing patterns that were in use even before the Ming Dynasty.

Whilst breaking new ground, *Mr. Dong and Mrs. Li* still follows the traditional pattern of Liyuan Opera, whose style and poetry remain attractive to audiences. The story is adapted from a modern novel about an old landlord, Mr. Peng, who doesn't trust his young wife, Mrs. Li. Before he dies, he asks the family teacher, Mr. Dong, to take charge of her. But Dong and Li fall in love.

The playwright Wang Renjie thoroughly understands the patterns of traditional poems and dramas. His work has clear characters, a simple structure, beautiful language and a fresh style. More importantly, he is very aware of the importance and charm of traditional operas. The combined efforts of Su Yanshuo, director of the Quanzhou Liyuan Opera League, and Zeng Jingping and Gong Wanli, the main performers, helped to enhance the inherent elegance and delicacy of the play.

Wang Renjie is a rare example of a playwright who has great respect for the historical and cultural value of local art. In a world of mass communication and diverse, contrasting cultures, the play integrates national tradition with more modern concerns. *Mr. Dong and Mrs. Li* is a classic in the field of traditional drama in modern China, representing the best of dramatic creations and performances in modern times.

From the beginning of the twenty-first century, influenced by UNESCO's global selection of intangible cultural heritage, hundreds of traditional Chinese operas have been supported and specially protected by central and local governments. Over a century earlier, dominated intentionally or otherwise by powerful

Intangible cultural heritage
In 1998, the United Nations Educational, Scientific and Cultural Organization (UNESCO) officially launched a project to protect oral and intangible cultural heritage. The project aimed to set up an international award for traditional national cultural art forms. Inspired by this, the protection of oral and intangible heritage in China has increased; many local operas which were on the point of extinction have now received more attention.

Western cultural values, Chinese opera tried to adapt oriental artistic traditions to the dramatic theories introduced by the West. This trend has changed markedly since the beginning of the twenty-first century. Chinese opera is, on the one hand, further integrating itself into the world, whilst on the other returning to its traditional operatic forms.

Appendix:
Chronological Table of the Chinese Dynasties

The Paleolithic Period	c.1,700,000–10,000 years ago
The Neolithic Period	c. 10,000–4,000 years ago
Xia Dynasty	2070–1600 BC
Shang Dynasty	1600–1046 BC
Western Zhou Dynasty	1046–771 BC
Spring and Autumn Period	770–476 BC
Warring States Period	475–221 BC
Qin Dynasty	221–206 BC
Western Han Dynasty	206 BC–AD 25
Eastern Han Dynasty	25–220
Three Kingdoms	220–280
Western Jin Dynasty	265–317
Eastern Jin Dynasty	317–420
Northern and Southern Dynasties	420–589
Sui Dynasty	581–618
Tang Dynasty	618–907
Five Dynasties	907–960
Northern Song Dynasty	960–1127
Southern Song Dynasty	1127–1276
Yuan Dynasty	1276–1368
Ming Dynasty	1368–1644
Qing Dynasty	1644–1911
Republic of China	1912–1949
People's Republic of China	Founded in 1949